BAKING AT THE
20TH CENTURY CAFE

BAKING AT THE 20TH CENTURY CAFE

Iconic European Desserts
from Linzer Torte to Honey Cake

MICHELLE POLZINE

with Jessica Battilana

PHOTOGRAPHS BY AYA BRACKETT

ARTISAN BOOKS | NEW YORK

Library of Congress Cataloging-in-Publication Data

Names: Polzine, Michelle, author. | 20th Century Cafe (San Francisco, Calif.) | Brackett, Aya, photographer.
Title: Baking at the 20th Century Cafe : iconic European desserts from linzer torte to honey cake / Michelle Polzine ; photographs by Aya Brackett.
Description: New York : Artisan Books, a division of Workman Publishing Co., Inc. [2020] | Includes index.
Identifiers: LCCN 2020016577 | ISBN 9781579658984 (hardcover)
Subjects: LCSH: Desserts. | Baking. | Cooking, European. | LCGFT: Cookbooks.
Classification: LCC TX773 .P65 2020 | DDC 641.86—dc23
LC record available at https://lccn.loc.gov/2020016577

Design by Suet Chong

Artisan books are available at special discounts when purchased in bulk for premiums and sales promotions as well as for fund-raising or educational use. Special editions or book excerpts also can be created to specification. For details, contact the Special Sales Director at the address below, or send an e-mail to specialmarkets@workman.com.

For speaking engagements, contact speakersbureau@workman.com.

Published by Artisan
A division of Workman Publishing Co., Inc.
225 Varick Street
New York, NY 10014-4381
artisanbooks.com

Artisan is a registered trademark of Workman Publishing Co., Inc.

Published simultaneously in Canada by Thomas Allen & Son, Limited

Printed in China

First printing, September 2020

1 3 5 7 9 10 8 6 4 2

For Franz,
who saw me rise from the dish pit
and fall down over and over and over.

Thanks, love.

I believe I will keep gettin' back up again.

CONTENTS

INTRODUCTION

Deposed royal families, world wars, and communist occupation have all left their mark on the former Austro-Hungarian Empire, but there, in the middle of Europe, the culture of cake still reigns supreme. Citizens of Vienna and Budapest think no more of having their afternoon coffee and pastry (*Jause*, which simply means snack) served on china with real silverware than most Americans think about grabbing a doughnut and a coffee in a paper cup to go. Pastry traditions that are centuries old are still part of daily life behind the doors of the grand cafes of central Europe. Glass cases are filled with beautiful cakes and pastries, including Sacher tortes, Dobos tortas, and all manner of schnitten, the precise cuts exposing what's inside: the practical artistry and craft that binds the past to the present and brings the flavors together in those beautiful layers. There's not a lot of florid, nonsensical decoration on these cakes. Instead, they display the careful construction that plays out in eating them: nut meringue layers, buttercreams, sponge cakes, whipped cream, thin chocolate glazes, crumbly, buttery pastry layers. With a few exceptions, what makes these pastries so grand are their components and how they are assembled. Although this kind of baking stems from a royal tradition, with a crescendo during the reign of the Hapsburgs, you may encounter cakes like these everywhere from Kansas to Kazakhstan!

Not to be outshone by their multilayered siblings are the beautiful fruit-topped pastries, streusel-covered kuchen, linzer tortes, and of course, *strudel*! Apple, cheese, poppy seed, and sour cherry strudel—in Budapest, there is a whole cafe dedicated entirely to strudel. Perhaps a little less "grand" but without compromise in construction or flavor are the smaller bites, like vanilla Kipferl, Linzer Augen, and little poppy seed–filled butter cookies, worthy of being served next to a gold-rimmed glass filled with Tokaji.

There is a vein of this tradition of European baking that runs through the baking in America today, especially in Jewish, eastern European, and the few old-time family bakeries that were once so common before bakeries in supermarket chains pushed many mom-and-pop shops out of business. It is the kind of baking that grandmas used to do, not just for special occasions but regularly, for Sunday dinner or when the grandkids came for a visit. This is the kind of baking that I love best and want to see a resurgence of. I say, make the cake you want and the occasion will happen! When I find a beautiful 1930s evening gown that fits me, I do not say to myself, "But I have nowhere to wear it!" I buy the dress and figure out the occasion to fit the outfit.

The Hungry American

When I took my first trip to central Europe, I was traveling as a tourist who happened to be a pastry chef. I love food, and I love eating, and the foods I love eating the most are desserts, so this has always played a big part in where the pins land on the map for prospective travel. In fact, it's really the only part. It's not that I don't enjoy sightseeing or museums, but to be frank, I see them as a means to build my appetite for the next meal. Travel is expensive, and time off does not come easily, so these excursions are few and far between, which means it is very important to maximize their content! When I lived on the East Coast, I liked to go to New York City for inspiration, for a long weekend. Now when my own San Francisco restaurant closes for a week in January, I try to get to Vienna and Budapest but sometimes only make it as far as Portland, Oregon. When travel isn't an option, I'll pick up a new cookbook (new to me; I collect vintage cookbooks) and visit wonderful places through the recipes and my own imagination. My feeling for Rick Rodgers's gift-from-the-pastry-gods *Kaffeehaus: Exquisite Desserts from the Classic Cafes of Vienna, Budapest, and Prague* is so strong that when I was presented with an offer to travel anywhere on earth by my brother, Ben, it was a given that I would choose to visit the former Austro-Hungarian Empire and experience the incredible baking of this confectionery wonderland.

My objective for the trip was to remain glamorous while stuffing my face with every schnitte, kuchen, and torte I could get my fat forints around. Having collected vintage clothing for more than twenty-five years, I had amassed a fairly respectable closet of beautiful old clothes, and by fairly respectable, I mean my wardrobe has its own room in my apartment. After years of watching movies starring Carole Lombard and Myrna Loy, with their innumerable overstuffed steamer trunks and nothing but a well-dressed dog to carry on the train platform, that was how I envisioned the start of my voyage to middle Europe!

Armed with Rick's book, I chose our first stop: Café Imperial in Nové Město, Prague's "new" part of town (there, "new" means the early twentieth century!). I wore my favorite 1930s knit jersey dress, hat, gloves, and silk coat with a fur collar. My companions and I stepped inside, and it was more amazing than I could have imagined. The entire place was filled with the most beautiful Art Nouveau tile work that I have ever seen. The pillars, the walls, the floors were covered with beautiful murals set in more tile! The ceiling—all tile! I had to dab my eyes with my handkerchief and take a few deep breaths before heading to our table. But something stopped me dead in my tiled tracks.

The pastry case! It was filled with both familiar and unknown sweets, and its marble top, covered with glass and silver cake stands, held even more unfamiliar, unpronounceable wonders. The cafe culture, so civilized, and so merciful to the novice; one simply needs to point, nod, and wait for the magic to appear. My companions stopped me after a great deal of this pointing and nodding, reminding me that this cafe was only the first of many stops.

The desserts, among them medovik (honey cake), Esterházy schnitten, and an apple strudel not so unlike the one I'd been struggling to create back home, were presented on gold-rimmed china, with beautiful silver forks. Our coffees were suitably dressed to complement their companions, served on little silver trays, with a demitasse spoon and a tiny glass of water on each one. As we sat there in a caffeinated, sugary stupor, sipping our coffees and tasting these time-tested treasures, things started to click for me. It was at this moment that my obsession with the cakes and tarts from this grand cafe tradition was born, and the seeds were planted for what would become my own little grand cafe, the 20th Century.

My Not-So-Grand Beginning

I began my life as a professional cook in Chapel Hill, North Carolina, after a most inauspicious start as a dishwasher. My bohemian notion of the very Zen act of dishwashing did not match up with the drudgery of hours spent bent over a sink. I did like the physical work, and the hours fit well with the schedule at the local punk rock club, the Cat's Cradle, but dishwashing was just too boring, and my little hummingbird brain longed for something more absorbing. Although I really liked cooking at home, and did lots of it, I'd never thought I could actually become a professional cook. Through some lucky punk rock connections (everything in Chapel Hill is connected to punk rock!), I managed to get a gig as the late-night cook/salad dressing maker at Pyewacket restaurant, which was a pretty fancy joint in those days.

I had arrived! I moved up the kitchen ranks, and I learned to cook, sort of—that is to say, I learned to cook from recipe cards. If I picked up techniques, it was more by accident than training; I wince when I think of how we weren't taught to season food. I think about our misguided musings about health food, how we operated as if salt and fat were bad. I did learn to work quickly, to organize my station for efficiency, and to maneuver in a very hot kitchen in close proximity to other people who were also moving quickly, with hot pans and knives. I learned about kitchen hierarchy and seniority, and how best to gain the esteem of my colleagues. There was great camaraderie and a healthy competition to see who could do more covers (entrées), and who could do the most prep for their coworkers.

I had some very good times cooking on the line, this kitchen being uncharacteristically full of women (and we used to cook in vintage dresses, not chef coats!), but I had always had a natural affinity and a certain awe for the sweet side of the kitchen. At Pyewacket, the pastry kitchen was a separate room, with its own walk-in, stove, and prep tables. I had baked quite a bit at home, and I was a member of a cookbook-of-the-month club, which delivered stories and recipes from restaurants in New York and San Francisco to me. Maybe it was Emily Luchetti, the renowned pastry chef of Stars, who, referring to her own switch from the savory to the sweet side of the kitchen, said, "At the end of the day, I would rather smell like chocolate and strawberries than garlic and shrimp!" She certainly had a point.

Then one lucky day—just like the plot device in a Broadway musical where the star can't go on and the eager understudy gets her big break—the bread baker was drunk, and I came to the rescue. Once I proved myself on the bread station, I was given a couple of the very coveted dessert baking shifts. I was in heaven! The desserts at Pyewacket were the strongest part of the menu. They were very simple but so good. The idea of low-fat or healthy never crossed into this sacred room. Regular menu items included black-bottom pie, lime sour cream pie, crème caramel, and chocolate cake divine (boy, was it ever!). I learned from my boss Julia Stockton (who was also responsible for many of the desserts in chef Bill Neal's cookbooks) how to use salt in desserts not only to enhance the flavor but also to bring flavor to the front of the palate by restraining the sugar. There is a real push and pull to bring everything into balance, and Julia had a true gift for hitting the "sweet spot." She was an incredible recipe developer, and this being my first dessert gig, I just assumed all pastry chefs wrote all of their own material. Sure, we used books, but more for reference and inspiration, not to be big copycats! Once, before I learned how to come up with my own recipes, I made a dessert from the Stars cookbook. It was for New Year's Eve, and it had, *ahem,* raspberries as the main ingredient. Said baker-about-town Sally Harmon, who, like any good Southern lady, could cut you to the quick with no effort, "Nothing excites people like fruit out of season!" Like a samurai, she sliced me in two. I had (and still have) so much to learn!

I worked at many restaurants, and was maybe a little too ambitious. I learned to drive at age twenty-nine just so I could go to work at Nana's in Durham, and I eventually became a pastry chef at a new restaurant called Elaine's, opened by Magnolia Grill alumnus Bret Jennings. As a pastry chef, I had to plan the menus, and I was determined to make them more seasonal. I tend toward extremes, though, and when I was looking back at some old menus recently, I realized that strawberries might star in as many as three desserts per menu, then the same thing with blueberries when they were in season, and then sour cherries. Sometimes the push for rapid personal growth makes me do some pretty dopey stuff. I soon learned that having nine desserts on my menu was diluting the impact of each one, when I could have just five, with no repeated featured ingredients, resulting in a menu that was more dynamic and could change more frequently. This shift toward seasonal ingredients led to my discovery of Lindsey Shere's classic book *Chez Panisse Desserts*

and an obsession with the Bay Area and all that perfect produce.

Having left San Francisco, where I was a political activist, in 1991 for North Carolina, where I had learned so much about food and baking, I now longed to return to the Bay Area with my new perspective as a pastry chef. After a couple of planes brought the World Trade Center to the ground, I figured World War III was coming and I'd better get back to San Francisco before we all were blown to smithereens. Upon my return, I found that nobody there had ever heard of Chapel Hill, Carrboro, or Durham, and that I would have to start at the bottom again; not dish-pit bottom, but pastry-ladder bottom. I was pretty frustrated working under pastry chefs whom I could mop the floor with, until I found my way to Delfina restaurant, where Jessica Cunningham hired me without being threatened by my experience or abilities.

We had fun together and made lots of desserts, and she had some nice stress-free vacations and someone to fill her shoes when she ran off to India for an indefinite period of time. I learned how to make simple, perfect desserts in mad quantities here, and I learned from Delfina's owner, Craig Stoll, that the person who gets a dessert that is not perfect doesn't care that the other 149 desserts you served that day were perfect; they care only about what is in front of them. This simple perspective had a tremendous impact on me, and it still does, every day.

It wasn't until I became the pastry chef of San Francisco's Range restaurant, though, that my skills, background, and creativity coalesced into something truly wonderful. Chef Phil West, for better or worse, let me have complete freedom, and I was able to build on and explore every sugary whim that popped into my head. I began to dabble in the central European pastry arts, and Phil was the person who encouraged me to set out on my own. (Today he is still the chef I hit up with all of my savory cooking queries.) An unobstructed faucet of creativity opened in me, and a totally organic, mad method of recipe developing began to flow through me. It's the same way I create recipes today, being open to inspiration from any damn thing but working through the creative process within a structure.

20th Century Cafe Baking

Since my excursions to the grand cafes of central Europe, creating and re-creating the experience of these visits in my own cafe has become my singular purpose in life, and on July 5, 2013, I turned the "Open" sign on the door around, without any announcement to the press, and then ran and hid behind the counter. From finding a corner location with the perfect light to sourcing just the right light fixtures and flooring, from agonizing over the color of the mohair for the banquette and how many feet the table bases should have, and from accidentally coming across the perfect tile for the bar to finding the quirkiest craftsperson in San Francisco to cut the edge on the marble countertop, piece by piece, I built my home. To say that running a cafe is my passion underscores the power it has over me; it is truly the work of my life. I'm still motivated by eating seasonally, but I think more often of how the season's offering can be presented as a torte rather than a plated dessert with multiple components. Still, I might throw some candied Meyer lemons and ground cardamom into a strudel as I'm filling it, or dust a date torte with pistachio praline to give it sparkle and crunch and put some coffee and orange in the dates themselves to highlight their natural flavor. I think of my method as a sneaky approach to making desserts that look simple but also delight the eater of the sweets in a way that will not be obvious to them.

Enter the honey cake: I did not invent it, but it is my version of this cake—the bestselling cake in the 20th Century Cafe canon of cakes—that has become one of the most famous cakes of the past decade. My secret weapon is the way I use the caramelization of the honey and condensed milk to highlight and intensify their inherent flavors while also creating entirely new flavors through the process. The acidity in the honey is heightened, and a delicious licorice quality comes through the darkly caramelized dulce de leche. Every time I make this cake, I still marvel at the complexity of the frosting, and every batch is just a little bit different. After seven years of making this cake, I'm still intrigued by a dessert with so much depth from so few ingredients. *Magic*, I say! I often sing the Olivia Newton-John song while building and frosting this cake, hoping no one is around when I get to the high notes.

The way I do things in the cafe, with very little mechanization and so much done by hand, taste, and eye, is a little bit silly for a business, but it will serve you well as you embark on this pastry adventure with me. For you at home, paying attention to every detail, ignoring the phone and your family, and emptying your purse to buy the finest ingredients is what I call "high-stakes baking"—these recipes don't mess around, and neither should you!

Cooking from This Book

As a fiction reader, I often used to rush to the end of the book to see what happened to our heroine, missing a lot of good writing and a lot of nuance in the plot. When you're working with this book, please don't do that! I insist that you read each recipe at least twice—that's right, *twice*—before you begin baking, and I mean all the way through, not skipping around to get to the juicy bits. Once you've finished making the recipe, or maybe while your cake layers are cooling, your dough is chilling, or you're in between turns, start taking notes, preferably in pencil in this book. I want you to write all over these pages! Try to refrain from giving me a mustache, but by all means, make lots of notations—scribbles, arrows, every little thing that will help you the next time you crack open the book. It will be hard to remember what you might have been thinking the last time you made a recipe, so spend a few minutes reflecting and taking notes.

I'm forever tweaking recipes to make them better, so I never consider anything as the final version. I think of a recipe as a living thing that needs to be allowed to change and grow. I promise you here that you have the most recent version of every recipe in the book, but the final one? There I promise nothing!

The recipes in the fruit and strudel chapters are organized seasonally. I owe much of my growth as a baker and a chef to my devotion to fruit, and to learning to observe and follow the seasons. The book begins with a chapter dedicated to fruit, because fruit is already a dessert itself, and baking with fruit is also a good place to learn a few critical baking techniques. The chapter includes some components that appear again in later chapters, like the crunch dough, almond cream, and dough for the date turnovers.

In the chapter featuring traditional and mostly traditional cakes and tortes, you'll learn to whip and fold meringue with the touch of an angel, spread batter like a sculptor, and stack cake layers like an architect. I hope you'll be inspired to put up your own preserves to make each of these recipes even more your own, and to furiously track down the best nuts and seeds you've ever tasted. The cake recipes are the ones that require the biggest time commitments, but if you go over them carefully before beginning, you'll see that I've often broken down the workload so you can make the recipes even if you don't have several hours in one day to dedicate to one dessert.

And for those strange people in your life who "don't really like dessert" (*what?!*), there are recipes for some wonderful treats. "Scones" with bacon, tarts made with vegetables, a savory crêpe cake, and naturally fermented bagels will satisfy the most curmudgeonly sweets haters of all.

Most of the recipes in this book come from the cafe menus, from special events, or from just plain kooky requests for desserts I've honored over the years. You'll find that many of the recipes contain no wheat flour, which makes them great for your gluten-avoiding friends. It also means you may need to scare up some ingredients that might not normally be in your pantry, such as tapioca flour and almond meal, but you'll be surprised at how easy it is to find these ingredients and at the wonderful structure and/or texture they add to your desserts!

I've listed some mail-order sources (see page 341) to assist if you can't find what you need locally. There is one particular chocolate—Valrhona's Coeur de Guanaja 80% cacao chocolate—that will be hard to do without for a couple of recipes. I feel slightly bad about doing this to you, but you'll probably have to mail-order it, or start bringing flowers or, better still, fruit to your favorite pastry chef so they will give you some. For the other ingredients, just use the freshest ones you can find, whether it's seeds, nuts, spices, flours, dairy products, or fruit. You might find yourself spending a day of your life making some of these recipes, and dammit, you want them to taste good, so it's worth a little extra expense!

Sometimes, no matter how much of a baking badass you are, things go wrong. Do not despair! If your cake cracks, or one of your layers breaks, you may scream in frustration and want to chuck it into the compost, but don't do it! Scream, yes, but after the screaming, put the broken layer(s) back together, strategically sandwiching them in between unbroken layers and using your filling or frosting as glue. Just yesterday, when *two* of my Mohnkuchen layers broke while I was taking them out of the pans with too much haste, I put them back together and it totally worked (with no one but you and me being the wiser).

Some of these recipes are going to require patience, but I hope that inspires an increasing love for the processes of baking; chopping, mixing, measuring, whipping, and folding properly; all are essential to your own baking success and enjoyment of this book. Just remember that the effort is worth the effort! Every detail, every bit of energy you put in, is going to pay off in your finished torte, tart, cake, or kuchen, and this will also make your next baking project, and the ones beyond it, better. Before you shop, take out your scale, and put on your finest vintage apron, be sure you understand the recipe as a whole, and have a plan for exactly how and when to tackle each component within the recipe. Now quit your dallying, and get to baking!

INGREDIENTS

Here is a list of some things you'll need to have in your pantry, including specific types or brands of commonly used ingredients and why they're your best options.

Almond Flour/Meal

Almond flour is typically made from blanched (skinless) almonds, and almond meal is made from almonds that still have their skins. The flour is generally more finely ground than the meal, but the two can be used interchangeably in the recipes in this book. Almond flour/meal is available at most grocery stores; if you don't use it frequently, store it in an airtight container in the freezer.

For the recipes in this book, and in my home kitchen and cafe, I use raw almond meal from Alfieri Farms (see Resources, page 341), but you can source one locally.

Almond Paste

Sold in tubes at most well-stocked grocery stores, almond paste is a combination of ground almonds and sugar. Note that almond paste is not the same thing as marzipan (though they are often sold in nearly identical packaging, stocked alongside each other in the grocery store, and confused by errand-running spouses on multiple occasions). Marzipan is sweeter and smoother, and the two cannot be used interchangeably.

Black Walnuts

Black walnuts are the old, wild tree nut that grows in the United States; English walnuts, by contrast, are almost all orchard-grown. But what really distinguishes the two is the flavor; black walnuts are rich and slightly tannic, and they have an almost grassy, floral flavor. The shells are very hard to crack, and thus most black walnuts are sold preshelled. I buy mine from Wine Forest Wild Foods (see Resources, page 341).

Buckwheat Flour

Although considered a grain, buckwheat is actually the seed of a flowering fruit, closely related to rhubarb, and is naturally gluten-free. It's ground into a gray-black flour that has a nutty, slightly bitter flavor and is used to made traditional Breton-style crêpes and classic blini. Store it in the refrigerator or freezer if you're keeping it for longer than 2 months.

Butter

Use unsalted butter for these recipes. You will be instructed to add salt where necessary.

Cacao Nibs

Small bits of crushed cacao beans, cacao nibs have a slightly bitter, nutty, chocolatey flavor. Many specialty grocery stores carry them now, but they are readily available online, and as with chocolate (see next page), Valrhona is a good source, as is World Wide Chocolate (see Resources, page 341).

Chestnut Flour

Made by grinding dry roasted chestnuts, this flour has a rich, nutty aroma and is naturally gluten-free. As with all nut flours, it can go rancid quickly, so purchase yours from a reputable market that sells through its stock rapidly—a health food store is a good place to look. It's also sold in many Italian grocery stores (labeled farina di castagna). Store chestnut flour in an airtight container in the refrigerator or freezer.

Chocolate

Do not scrimp when buying chocolate. I call for two varieties in this book: Valrhona Araguani, which is a 72% cacao chocolate (in smaller bars, it's called Grand Cru Araguani), and Valrhona Coeur de Guanaja, which is an 80% cacao chocolate. (The percentage indicates how much cacao is in the chocolate but does not distinguish between cocoa butter and cocoa solids.) Both of these come in the form of "fèves," which are pretty little oval disks, woefully easy to snack on. (If you aren't using fèves or disks of chocolate, you will need to chop the chocolate for each recipe, or just chop the whole block when you open it, so it's ready to go.) I've used Valrhona for decades, and I find their chocolate to be consistent, reliable, and delicious. Any high-quality chocolate with a similar percentage can be used in place of the Araguani chocolate, but the Coeur de Guanaja is unique. It is formulated specifically with a lower fat content (less cocoa butter and more cocoa solids) for use in recipes where cocoa would give the desired intensity but the smoothness of chocolate is needed for texture. Valrhona chocolate can be purchased online (see Resources, page 341).

Coconut

Except when I want strips or larger "chips" of coconut to garnish a cake or dessert, I always use finely shredded unsweetened dried coconut, sometimes called macaroon coconut. Although I have gone out into my backyard, busted open a coconut, and grated the meat for a cake, I'm not making you do that. Keep in mind that since the coconut is fine and dry, it will toast *very* quickly.

Dates

One of the many lovely things about living in San Francisco is proximity to the date farms of Southern California. At my farmers' markets, I can choose from among a dozen different varieties of dates, from syrupy Barhi and Deglet Noor to the large, firm, maple-y Medjools, which are the variety that seem to make their way most often to grocery stores elsewhere. Medjools are fine, and they will work for all the recipes in this book that call for dates. The handpicked ones from Rancho Meladuco are especially good; for the coveted Barhi and other varieties, including Medjools, order from Flying Disc Ranch (see Resources, page 341).

Dried Plums

The recipes for Plum Lekvar (page 77) and the strudel with chocolate, plums, and hazelnuts (see page 255) call for dried plums. While prunes are one type of dried plum, for these recipes I'm referring to another type, one that more closely resembles dried apricots or peaches and has much less sweetness and higher acidity. I'm partial to the dried plums from Blossom Bluff Orchards, which can be ordered online (see Resources, page 341).

Dried Sour Cherries

The sour cherries I use are lightly sweetened dried Montmorency cherries from Michigan, the largest producer of sour cherries in the United States, but there are many other varieties. If you happen to live in an area where you can get fresh sour cherries, sometimes called pie cherries, I strongly urge you to dedicate a day or two of your life every year to making your own sour cherry jam, and to bring me some when you visit San Francisco. I'll buy you a drink!

Flour

For the recipes in this book, cake and pastry flour can be used interchangeably, although there is a slight difference between them. When I call for bread flour, I'm referring to high gluten bread flour that contains 14% to 15% protein. Although a lower-protein (12.5%) bread flour will work (the recipes were tested with both), the breads will have quite a bit more loft with the higher-protein version, so get it if you can. When testing the recipes, I used the method of lightly sprinkling the flour into the cup and leveling it with the edge of an offset spatula or the straight edge of a butter knife, and you should too. Flour is the trickiest ingredient there is to get consistent results with when using volume measures, so if you've considered buying a digital kitchen scale, *do it now!*

Gelatin

I always use bronze-strength sheet gelatin (the silver and gold can be substituted sheet for sheet for the bronze, but not by weight), instead of powdered gelatin, to set custards and puddings. It's easier and less messy to work with. No dissolving required; just put it in some ice water to soften it (it can hang out in the ice water for up to an hour if you get distracted, or have to arrest your baking to attend to other matters!), then squeeze out the excess liquid and throw it into the warm liquid in your recipe. It also yields more consistent results than powdered gelatin. (A standard conversion for powdered gelatin is 1 envelope = 3 sheets leaf gelatin.) True, it's not as easy to find as the powdered, but it can be ordered online (see Resources, page 341) or found in specialty baking shops, and it will keep forever in your pantry—buy a bunch, so you'll always have it at the ready.

Leaves: Rose Geranium, Lemon Verbena, and Fig or Peach Leaves

A couple of the recipes in this book call for rose geranium, lemon verbena, or fig or peach leaves. I'm not trying to frustrate you by calling for these ingredients, which I know cannot be purchased at any grocery store. Rather, I hope that curiosity gets the best of you and you seek out these aromatic leaves, perhaps by asking a friend with a garden, or inquiring about them with a grower at the farmers' market or orchard you frequent. Or, in the case of the rose geranium or lemon verbena, trying your hand at growing your own, as both are quite easy to propagate, and even I, with my brown thumb and close proximity to a major freeway, have managed to keep a robust rose geranium bush!

Nigella Seeds

Used in many cuisines, including Transylvanian, these tiny black, teardrop-shaped seeds, sometimes referred to as Russian caraway (though they are not related to caraway at all), have a flavor that hints at oregano and roasted onion. Use them to top bagels, alone or as part of an "everything" mix (see page 312), or to top knishes (see page 271) in place of the poppy seeds. You can purchase them online (see Resources, page 341).

Nuts

Many of these recipes call for nuts, and, as with the other ingredients in this section, starting with good quality is the first order; proper storage is the second.

I get all my nuts from my local farmers' market or order them directly from the farm. I like to support other small businesses, and I like direct sourcing when I can, but the best reason for buying this way is that the quality of the nuts really comes through in these recipes, and good nuts will elevate your baking.

I store all my nuts in airtight containers in the refrigerator, but you can keep them in the freezer if you have a large quantity that you aren't going to get through within a few months. High-quality nuts don't need to have much done to them—which means, please don't ruin them by toasting the crap out of them! I prefer to toast mine at a lower temperature than many recipes call for, 325°F (165°C), certainly no higher than 350°F (175°C), for 8 to 15 minutes, depending on the nut and whether the recipe calls for "lightly toasted" or "toasted" nuts. In a case where removing the sweetness from the nuts is desired, you can take them darker, being careful just to caramelize the sugars in the nuts without burning the oils. The best "toaster tester" is your nose!

When you first smell the nuts, they are lightly toasted. After 3 or 4 more minutes, they are "toasted," and 2 or 3 minutes after that, they are well toasted; 3 or 4 minutes after that, they are just toast. When grinding toasted nuts for cakes, make sure they have cooled completely, or you may end up making very fancy nut butter!

Oloroso Sherry

Made from a fortified wine that has oxidized, Oloroso is darker and nuttier than Amontillado sherry, and it is fortified at an earlier stage, so it lacks the fresh, yeasty flavor of Fino sherries. I use it in the Kávé Becsípett Sherry Trifle on page 163.

Poppy Seeds

You must be very discerning about your poppy seeds. In most of the baking we do in America, these tiny round seeds are treated almost as an afterthought, added to the batter for a lemon cake, or maybe to a salad dressing for some crunch, so no wonder they are relegated to the unrefrigerated section of most grocery stores. But those questionable seeds will simply not do for these recipes! If you cannot find a store that sells poppy seeds refrigerated or frozen and keeps their stock rotated, do not buy them, as no good will come of it. Once, I was grinding the seeds for the Mohnkuchen (page 97), and the seeds smelled a little like Play-Doh. I didn't listen to the voice in my head that tried to stop me, and I made the cake anyway, only to have to chuck the whole thing into the compost bin after tasting it. So try to smell before you buy; if the seeds smell stale, look elsewhere. Because poppy seeds have a high oil content, they should always be refrigerated or frozen. But they actually keep for months if stored properly, so your worries are over once you find a good source. Try your local co-op or health food store. Or, for a good online source, try Penzeys (see Resources, page 341).

Rose Water

Rose water is exactly what it sounds like: water in which rose petals have been steeped. It has a wonderful fragrance and flavor, and a little goes a long way (too much, and your dessert may taste like soap). It's available at many grocery stores (look in the problematically named "International" aisle), in specialty baking shops, and online; Nielsen-Massey is a good brand (see Resources, page 341).

Salt

Almost without exception, I used Diamond Crystal brand kosher salt in the recipes in this book (the exceptions are the fine sea salt I call for in bread recipes, and Maldon salt, a beautiful finishing sea salt with prismatic crystals, which I use as a garnish). You might decide to use another salt, but please know that these recipes were developed and tested with Diamond Crystal kosher, and that other brands and types of salt cannot be subbed in equally. For example, a teaspoon of, say, Morton's kosher salt, which is much coarser, is not the same as a teaspoon of Diamond Crystal.

Sourdough Starter

Got a friend or coworker who is an avid baker? Ask them to give you a little of their starter. Otherwise, starting your own culture (see page 310) is easy,

theoretically at least, but if for whatever reason, you lack the time, energy, or necessary native microbes to start your own, you can purchase sourdough starter online (see Resources, page 341). Keep in mind that your starter will change, becoming dominated by the cultures that live in your kitchen. Remember, it's not where the culture is from that matters, it's where it's at.

Sugar

I call for a number of different types of sugar throughout this book. Many of the recipes call for granulated sugar, and I always use cane sugar (not beet sugar). Demerara sugar is a large-grain cane sugar with an amber color and a mild, toffee-like flavor; it's often used as a sanding sugar. Turbinado sugar, also called raw cane sugar, is a coarse light brown sugar. It comes from the first pressing of the sugarcane and is less processed than white sugar, with a deeper, richer flavor. Muscovado sugar is another unrefined cane sugar. It's as fine and moist as brown sugar, but unlike brown sugar, which is just white sugar with molasses added, it has lots of minerals and a much deeper, darker flavor. It's available in two varieties, light and dark, but the recipes in this book all call for light.

Tapioca Flour

I use tapioca flour, which is naturally gluten-free, frequently in cakes and to thicken fruit desserts. Look for a brand derived from cassava (some "tapioca" flours are made from different, though similar, plants, but aren't exactly the same). Thanks to the explosive rise of gluten-free baking, tapioca flour can now be found in most grocery stores;

Bob's Red Mill is a widely available brand (see Resources, page 341).

Yeast

At the typical grocery store, you have two choices for yeast: active dry and instant. Active dry has larger granules and must be dissolved in a warm liquid (proofed) before using, while instant can be added directly to the flour in the recipe without being dissolved first. You can substitute active dry yeast for instant; use 25 percent more active dry (for example, if a recipe calls for 1 teaspoon instant, use 1¼ teaspoons active dry). But there is a third variety of yeast, variously known as cake, compressed, or fresh yeast, which is what I typically use; it is soft and crumbly, requires no proofing, and dissolves easily. It is, however, quite perishable, and must be kept refrigerated. Fresh yeast can be found in the bulk section of many health food stores, such as your local co-op. The recipes in this book that call for yeast give measurements for both fresh yeast and instant.

LIQUID CONVERSIONS

Here is a chart of some commonly used liquid ingredients and a basic conversion for each. This information may differ from other charts out there, but these are my measurements, determined with my trusty Pyrex measure, a kitchen scale, and measuring spoons!

Water	100 milliliters = 100 grams	1 cup = 230 grams	1 tablespoon = 14 grams
Whole milk	100 milliliters = 100 grams	1 cup = 230 grams	1 tablespoon = 14 grams
Buttermilk	100 milliliters = 100 grams	1 cup = 230 grams	1 tablespoon = 14 grams
Heavy cream	100 milliliters = 96 grams	1 cup = 220 grams	1 tablespoon = 14 grams
Oil	100 milliliters = 86 grams	1 cup = 200 grams	1 tablespoon = 12 grams
Honey	100 milliliters = 144 grams	1 cup = 328 grams	1 tablespoon = 20 grams

EQUIPMENT

Baking is easier when you have the right tools. This doesn't mean you need loads of specialty equipment to execute the recipes in the book, just that a few well-chosen items will make life easier and will make your recipes turn out better. This list of equipment is divided into two categories: Must-Haves and Might-Haves. You'll also find specific equipment called out at the beginning of each chapter.

MUST-HAVES

Digital Scale

It is annoying but true that baking is a more precise science than savory cooking. (I don't make the rules; I just follow them!) To get accurate measurements that will ensure that your recipes are going to work, you need a small digital kitchen scale. Yes, the recipes will *work* with the volume measurements listed, but this is an advanced baking book; you may spend your whole day on one dessert, and I think you want more out of your baking than a recipe merely "working." Personally, I baked as a professional for years without a scale, but I was using recipes that I wrote myself, with a pen and with the same hands that were used to measure the flour. A cup of flour using the sprinkle-and-level method is always the same for me, but it may not be the same for you. Not only does working with a scale guarantee that the results are always, always the same, no matter the weather, the baker, or any other variables, but it also is actually faster and easier to weigh your ingredients, and doing so uses fewer pieces of equipment. You'll thank me when cleanup time comes. If you invest in only one piece of equipment to make the recipes in this book, let it be a trusty digital scale. It needn't be fancy or expensive; look for one that can toggle between ounces and grams, that can weigh amounts up to 5 pounds (2.5 kilograms), and that has a removable plate, which makes cleaning easier.

Large Metal Mixing Bowls

Look for stainless steel bowls that are wider than they are deep. I call these my "folding" bowls because that's primarily what I use them for. I love using my vintage bowls for baking, but I do feel a little nervous about possible lead in the glaze!

Large Rubber Spatulas

Many of the recipes in this book require folding egg whites into batter, which is much easier to do if you have a large rubber spatula. Get a couple, making sure at least one is heatproof, and never, ever use the same ones for baking and for savory cooking, because they easily pick up off flavors, and you don't want your cake batter tasting like garlic!

Liquid Measuring Cup

Although I firmly stand by my previous testimonial about the scale, I usually prefer to use a volume measure for liquids (breads and strudel dough being exceptions to this rule). Don't kill me, but different fat levels in your liquid dairy, for example, will affect the weight! Water, while supplies last, is always the same, thank god. I love my trusty Pyrex glass measure; it has ounces and cups as well as milligrams, and I can pour hot stuff into it without fear of toxic chemicals from plastic leaching into my food. Never use a liquid measuring cup for dry ingredients!

Mesh Sieves

A simple, inexpensive mesh sieve can do double duty as a sifter (for dry ingredients) and a strainer (for liquid mixtures, like custards). You will need a sieve with a more open screen, or an old-fashioned sifter, for recipes made with almond meal.

Offset Spatulas

My small offset spatula (which I nicknamed "Baby") is one of my most useful tools. I use it to smooth cake batters in their pans, to help me unmold baked cakes, and for other tasks too myriad to name. Get a large one, which is useful for finishing cakes, as well as a small one.

Round Cake Pans

A couple of heavy 9-by-3-inch (23-by-8-centimeter) round anodized aluminum cake pans are an essential investment. The depth is especially important; with a shallower pan, your cake may overflow or dome dramatically.

Sheet Pans (aka Rimmed Baking Sheets)

Many of the cakes in this book are baked in quarter sheet pans (9 by 13 inches/23 by 33 centimeters) or half sheet pans (18 by 13 inches/46 by 33 centimeters). These are also what you need for the cookies, bagels, and many other recipes. Buy sturdy heavy-duty 18-gauge aluminum pans with rolled edges, not those thin, chintzy ones that warp if you look at them wrong. These pans are not expensive, so you can replace them when they get gross. When the recipes here (and in most other cookbooks) refer to a "sheet pan," it is actually a half sheet pan we mean; most home ovens aren't big enough for a full sheet pan.

Stand (or Handheld) Mixer

While some of the recipes in the book are made by hand, many require a mixer. A stand mixer is my choice for mixing cookie doughs and cake batters and for beating egg whites to snowy peaks. A handheld mixer will generally work, but note that these recipes were developed with a stand mixer, so you'll likely have to beat your ingredients longer than specified if using a handheld mixer, and you will also be asked to incorporate the dry or more delicate ingredients by hand.

Tart Pans

I love the shallow fluted tart pans with removable bottoms. Not only are these essential for a pretty linzer torte, but the pan bottoms are one of my favorite tools in the kitchen! I slide them under delicate torte layers to stack them when a spatula would be too small, to assist in flipping cheesecakes out of pans and back onto their crusts, and to transfer a finished cake or tart to a serving platter when I wouldn't trust even the biggest burger spatula in my kitchen for such a job.

Thermometer

For around $35, you can purchase a high-quality instant-read thermometer, or for around $10 or less, a simple analog one; either will ensure that you never overcook your ice cream base again.

Whisk

An 8-inch (20-centimeter) balloon whisk is perfect for whipping cream and for beating egg whites by hand when you have too few to beat in the bowl of a stand mixer. In some instances, I use my balloon whisk for folding, too, as well as for whisking custards and the like.

Wire Rack

In many of the recipes, you will be instructed to transfer to a wire rack and cool; if you don't have one, don't despair! Just place a sheet pan on the counter and set the hot pan perpendicular to the empty one. All you are trying to do is get some air circulation under the hot pan. You should see some of the feats of balance I've achieved!

MIGHT-HAVES

Blender

When making any of the recipes that contain ground poppy seeds (for example, the Mohnkuchen on page 97), the single best way to grind them is in a blender.

Food Mill

This is a handy tool for ricing potatoes, sieving apples for apple butter, or milling the seeds out of raspberry or blackberry preserves. It's also a piece of equipment that is easily found in a thrift store. If you can find one with multiple disks, oh baby!

Food Processor

Though you can certainly make cookie crumbs (see Crumbs, page 35) without a food processor, and with enough time and patience you could probably (maybe) reduce nuts by hand to a texture similar to what a food processor can achieve, this appliance is a worthwhile investment, since it can do those tasks and many, many more quickly and easily. If you're going to bother getting one, don't waste your money on a tiny prep-size one; get a full-size food processor, because you'll soon discover how useful it is, both for baking tasks and for savory cooking. I found mine at the thrift store, so stop in the kitchen section when passing by.

Pizza Pans

Flat pizza pans are cheap; at 12 inches (30.5 centimeters), they don't take up much space, and they surely will ease your burden when you make any of the tarts in this book.

Ramekins

To try your hand at the recipe for Cranberry-Ginger Upside-Down Cakes (page 67), invest in a set of 8-ounce (237-milliliter) or 6-ounce (178-milliliter) ceramic ramekins. The Chocolate Soufflés (page 177) are made in 6-ounce (178-milliliter) ramekins. You can also make the Meyer Lemon Pudding Cake (page 69) or either of the other upside-down cakes (see pages 51 and 57) in individual portions if you want to be fancy.

FRUIT
DESSERTS

Fruit is the best ingredient in all dessert land. You may protest, "But I'm a chocolate person!" Well, chocolate person, chocolate is a fruit too! And while we're at it, so is coffee.

My first true awakening as a pastry chef happened because of a fruit dessert. A proper fruit dessert showcases the skill not only of the cook but of the grower too, and it is most likely to evoke memories of home in all of us. The pride of the foods grown in our homelands, ancestral or adopted, is something we all share. Folks from the southern United States brag about their peaches, those from England about their apples, and people from Hungary about their cherries, and I've been privy to some heated arguments refuting such supremacy! I recently had a few pedigree-free apricots come to me from the backyard of a friend: Were they the best apricots I've ever tasted? Yes! Can this opinion be trusted as objective? No!

It's true that if you want to make the best fruit desserts, you have to start with the best fruit. I know you've heard this a million times, but you must stay true to the course. We've all been guilty of seeing a fruit recipe we want to make, then shopping for it and just going with the best we can find, buying the fruit out of season, maybe, or knowing it might not be quite ripe enough.

I urge you to start thinking about it the other way around. If you want to make a fruit dessert tonight, go shopping first, and then choose what to make based on what you find. If you see some gorgeous apricots or nectarines that need another day or two on the counter, buy them anyway, and plan what you'll make when they're ready. Believe me, you're much better off holding ripe fruit in your refrigerator for a couple of days than you are expecting your oven to magically transform underripe specimens into loving spoonfuls of ambrosia!

One more piece of tactical advice: If you're looking for top-shelf produce, it helps to shop at the farmers' market. There you are liable to find more interesting varieties of truly ripe fruit. And if you become a loyal customer, the farmers may tip you off to something special, like their last flat of sour cherries, perfect pints of jewel-like red currants, or maybe some fruit that's too ugly to display but tastes like heaven. While we're trained to judge by appearance, keep in mind that sometimes the most flavorful fruit is not the best looking.

You will find recipes in this chapter for all kinds of fruit desserts, along with little tips for winging it if you have a different fruit from what a recipe calls for. Honestly, any of the tarts, upside-down cakes, and cobblers can be tweaked to accommodate different fruits. It's a little like jazz; first we learn the standards, and then, if we keep at it, one day we'll be flying like Bird.

Skills and Equipment

In this chapter, you will make long crusts (puff pastry–like turnover dough) and short crusts (shortbread-like dough), doughs marbled with butter (the Crunch Dough), and delicious old-fashioned cakes using the same creaming method your grandmother used to get that batter as fluffy as a cloud. For these doughs, you won't need much more than a rolling pin and a scale. For the cakes, a stand mixer is a big help. If you have just a handheld one with the double rotary blades, use that for creaming the butter and incorporating the eggs, but then fold in the flour and liquids by hand. One pan called for here that you may not have is a 9-by-3-inch (23-by-8-centimeter) round cake pan; some of the single-layer cakes can get pretty exuberant, and using this deeper pan is an extra precaution against possible spillover in the oven. I have a particular love for quarter sheet pans; their smaller size means they will fit in even the tiniest oven, and it's easy to spread batters evenly in them. And because they are so small, they tend to bake cakes and tarts more evenly than a half sheet pan would.

If you want to make jam, think about buying a copper pot. Copper is a great conductor of heat and helps the pectin gel, and it's so pretty that it will make these projects much more fun.

A nice sharp paring knife is essential for cutting ripe fruit into perfect wedges, and I have both a sweet and a savory cutting board at home. If you have only one, keep one side strictly for fruit, mark it with a Sharpie, and be prepared to police the other members of your household; I've found that threatening to withhold the sweets you are making is pretty effective.

RHUBARB TART WITH SOUR CHERRY LEKVAR

*Makes one 12-inch
(30.5-centimeter) tart;
serves 8*

1 recipe Crunch Dough (recipe follows)

FOR THE FILLING

2 tablespoons fine dry cookie, cake, or bread crumbs (see Crumbs, page 35)

2 tablespoons plus 1 teaspoon (17.5 grams) all-purpose flour

1 cup (260 grams) Sour Cherry Lekvar (recipe follows)

¼ cup plus 3 tablespoons (87 grams) sugar, plus more for sprinkling

Pinch of kosher salt

1 pound (454 grams) rhubarb, trimmed and cut into 2- to 3-inch (5- to 8-centimeter) pieces

1 tablespoon (14 grams) unsalted butter, melted

Spring is my favorite season for vegetables, but for a pastry chef, the season can be pretty disheartening. In restaurants where I have worked, I'd look on jealously as the savory cooks would taunt me with their fresh spring peas, artichokes, and fava beans while I'd be trying to coax the magic out of faded citrus and dried fruit. Rhubarb to the rescue! Some chefs think they're too good to use hothouse rhubarb and will wait for the field-grown, but not me. Gimme that hot-pink rhubarb.

If you have a pizza stone, by all means use it here, and in that case, make sure you preheat your oven for a good hour to ensure that your tart will develop a crisp, golden bottom that can stand up to all the juicy fruit. If you haven't got one, though, don't despair! You can bake your tart either directly on the floor of the oven or on the bottom rack. You can also try baking it on the oven floor for the first 15 minutes, until the bottom of the crust is well browned, and then moving it to the lowest shelf for the last 25 minutes. It will take making this tart or the Strawberry Tart (page 39) once or twice to find the sweet spot in your oven, so please make any notations directly on these pages. This will make baking future tarts easier and stress-free.

Adding some kind of moisture barrier (such as dry cookie, cake, or plain bread crumbs) between the fruit and the dough also helps prevent a soggy crust. I've tried to sidestep this and had some pretty mediocre results, so don't skip this part; the barrier is critical (see Crumbs, page 35).

Making this dough employs a crazy technique adapted from one I learned at Chez Panisse. By crazy, I mean you have to suspend disbelief to make the dough, but the method I use yields a dough that is marbled, instead of spotted with butter, so the fat doesn't melt out during baking, leaving holes that would release juices and cause the crust to become soggy. The finished crust is crispy, flaky, and delicate but somehow sturdy enough to support all that rhubarb.

1. On a lightly floured work surface, with a lightly floured rolling pin, roll the dough to a 12-inch (30.5-centimeter) circle, then extend the outer ¾ inch (2 centimeters) of the circle, rolling it a little thinner, until the dough is 13 inches (33 centimeters) in diameter. Transfer to a parchment-lined round pizza pan or baking sheet big enough to hold the tart and refrigerate until very firm, about 45 minutes.

(continued)

2. Arrange an oven rack in the bottom third of the oven, place a pizza stone on it, if using, and preheat the oven to 425°F (220°C).

3. **MAKE THE FILLING:** In a small bowl, combine the crumbs and 1 teaspoon of the flour. Remove the chilled dough from the refrigerator, slide the dough, still on the parchment, back to the counter, and, with an offset spatula, spread the cherry lekvar all over the dough, leaving a ½-inch (1.5-centimeter) border. Sprinkle the crumb-flour mixture over evenly and pat gently so the crumbs stick to the lekvar. Slide the dough, still on the parchment, back onto the pan, and return the dough to the refrigerator.

4. In a small bowl, mix together the remaining 2 tablespoons (15 grams) flour, ¼ cup plus 2 tablespoons (75 grams) of the sugar, and the salt; set aside. Cut each piece of rhubarb lengthwise into thin batons, ⅛ to ¼ inch (0.3 to 0.5 centimeter) thick (like sticks of gum!) and transfer to a large bowl. Remove the dough from the fridge.

5. Dump the sugar mixture into the bowl with the rhubarb and toss very quickly to coat. Working as quickly as possible, layer the rhubarb evenly all over the tart, making pretty crisscrosses, up to the edges of your crumb barrier; I find it helps to make a rhubarb corral at the edges of the circle to contain my placement, and that's where I put the least pink pieces, since they will be covered by dough. Fold the edges of the tart over, twisting the dough loosely under itself (the cherry lekvar will create a filling for this part, much like as in a stuffed-crust pizza!) and forming a rope-shaped edge. Brush the finished edge with the melted butter and sprinkle with the remaining tablespoon of sugar.

6. Transfer the tart to the bottom rack (on top of the pizza stone, if using) or the floor of the oven and bake for 15 minutes. Meanwhile, cut a parchment circle 11 inches (28 centimeters) in diameter and, with scissors or the tip of a sharp knife, cut some slits into the circle (kind of like making a paper snowflake). Set aside.

7. After the tart has baked for 15 minutes, set the parchment round directly on top of it, covering the fruit but not the crust; this will keep the fruit from drying out in the hot oven. Bake until the rhubarb is all bubbly and the crust is a dark golden brown, 35 to 40 minutes. Check on the tart occasionally to make sure the bottom isn't getting too dark (although this

is unlikely). If it is, move the tart off the pizza stone, if using, or off the floor of the oven and onto a higher rack. Remove the tart from the oven and let cool for a moment, then grab the edges of the parchment and, in one swift motion, slide the tart off the pan onto a wire rack to cool. This is scary, but don't be scared: You can do it! Or, if your pan has edges, cool the tart on the pan and then use the flat bottom of a removable-bottomed tart pan, sliding it under the tart, to transfer it to a serving plate or cutting board. (You can also just cut it on the pan, but don't use your best knife.)

8. Cut the tart into wedges and serve plain, with Whipped Cream (page 330), or with Cardamom Ice Cream (page 180) and Rose Geranium Syrup (page 340). This tart is best eaten the day it's made.

Crumbs

A number of recipes in this book call for crumbs, which act as a moisture barrier, preventing juicy fillings from making your pastry soggy. What you use for these crumbs depends on what you have around—you really can use almost anything, including cookies, cake scraps, stale bread, even leftover unfilled cream puffs. Simply dry out your whatever-you-have-on-hand in a low oven, then blitz in a food processor or crush with a rolling pin. Store-bought graham crackers, amaretti, or shortbread cookies can also be used. If crumbs are called for in a savory recipe (such as Potato Knishes, page 271, or Moldovan Cheese and Nettle Pie, page 277), use dry bread or cracker crumbs.

Although weights are given for the crumbs in these recipes, note that exact weights are not possible. Size, composition, and humidity are all factors here! So I will ask you to use your own judgment. And if your fruit is very juicy, or your filling seems wet, use an extra scattering of crumbs. Leftover crumbs can be stored in the freezer.

Crunch Dough

*Makes enough for
one 12-inch
(30.5-centimeter) tart*

8 tablespoons (113 grams) cold unsalted butter

1 cup (120 grams) all-purpose flour

½ teaspoon sugar

¼ teaspoon kosher salt

¼ cup (59 milliliters) ice-cold water

By the time I started working at Chez Panisse, I had baked a goodly number of pies and tarts, but I had never seen a dough like this. Demonstrated to the Chez cooks many generations before my time by chef Jacques Pépin, it was the dough we used every single day in our tarts for the cafe. As a budding baker, I'd had it drilled into me since day one that a flaky dough can only be achieved by using cold fat. *Au contraire, ma soeur!* For this dough, you use soft butter; not as soft as when making cookies, but soft enough so that when you squeeze the cubes of butter gently, they feel elastic and don't crack when you pinch their sides. If making this dough on a hot day, you might have to take your butter in and out of the fridge a few times to get that perfect moment when the butter is slightly yielding but not overly complacent. You'll know your butter has missed the mark if it starts to look a little oily. Pop the cubes back into the fridge for a minute or two, and you'll be back in business. This dough is light, flaky, crispy, and, well, crunchy!

1. Cut the butter into 16 equal cubes, set aside on parchment or waxed paper, and let come to cool room temperature. In a medium deep bowl (such as the bowl of a stand mixer), combine the flour, sugar, and salt.

2. When a cube of butter feels somewhat plasticky but doesn't crack when you squeeze it, throw all the pieces into the bowl with the dry ingredients and toss them in the flour to coat. Using your hands, toss the butter and flour around to knock the corners off the butter cubes (this step coats the flour with a little bit of butter, just enough to keep the dough tender). Next, push all the chunks to one side of the bowl and, working methodically but quickly, flatten each piece between your fingertips into a "tongue" and toss it to the other side of the bowl. Toss again to distribute the butter throughout the flour.

3. Splay the fingers of your dominant hand out, fingers pointed down over the bowl, and pour the ice water down the back of your hand, creating a little fountain. (Yes, it's really cold.) Then bend your fingers until your hand resembles a claw and rake the dough, moving back and forth very quickly to distribute the water throughout the dough and work the butter in.

(continued)

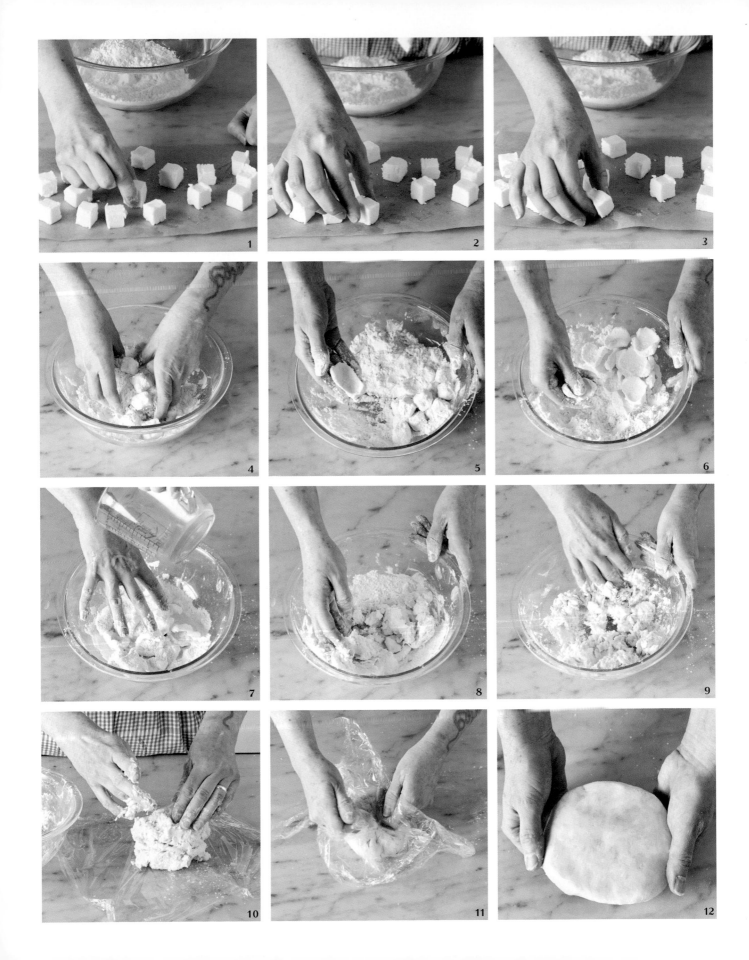

4. Once the dough is shaggy but with no dry spots, continue raking to pull it together into a ball (if the dough still seems dry, sprinkle over additional ice water, up to 1 tablespoon, until it's a shaggy mass), then transfer to a sheet of plastic wrap. Pull two opposite sides of the plastic wrap over the dough and use the plastic to push the sides of the dough in toward the center, then rotate the dough 180 degrees and repeat six more times, to get that wonderful marbled texture. Pull the plastic wrap tightly around the dough and flatten it into a disk ¾ to 1 inch (2 to 2.5 centimeters) thick. Chill for at least an hour before rolling, or wrap well and freeze for up to 2 months; thaw overnight in the refrigerator or at room temperature until defrosted but still cool before using.

Sour Cherry Lekvar

Makes 1 cup
(260 grams)

Scant 1 cup (140 grams) dried sour cherries (see page 19)

½ cup (118 milliliters) water, plus more as needed

2 tablespoons (24 grams) sugar

The best cherries I've found for this lekvar, which is a thick jam-like filling, are dried Montmorency sour cherries from Michigan. If you want to make a big batch, puree it in a food processor rather than chopping it by hand, and store it in an airtight container in the fridge, with parchment or waxed paper pressed directly against the surface of the lekvar. It will keep this way for at least a month.

1. Combine the cherries, water, and sugar in a small saucepan and bring to a simmer over medium-high heat. Then turn off the heat, cover, and let stand for about an hour, until the cherries are soft.

2. Return the mixture to a simmer over medium-high heat and simmer until most of the liquid has reduced. Let cool slightly, then transfer to a cutting board and finely chop, or puree in a food processor. Transfer to a jar or other container and let cool completely before using.

STRAWBERRY TART

*Makes one 12-inch
(30.5-centimeter) tart;
serves 8*

1 recipe Crunch Dough
(page 36)

FOR THE FILLING

¼ cup (28 grams) dry cookie
or cake crumbs (see Crumbs,
page 35)

2 tablespoons (15 grams) all-
purpose flour

¾ cup (170 grams) Almond
Cream (recipe follows), at room
temperature

1½ pounds (680 grams) small
strawberries, halved (see Note)

1 tablespoon (14 grams)
unsalted butter, melted and
cooled

¼ cup (50 grams) sugar

Cooked strawberries can be mushy, but in this tart, the long exposure to the oven heat pulls out the moisture and concentrates the juices, making the berries instead slightly chewy and intense. There is a good deal of knife work and arranging involved for this tart, so give yourself plenty of time to make it (the almond cream can be made well in advance and refrigerated or frozen until you're ready to bake the tart). If you've got the space, put your tart shell in the freezer while you prep the berries so the dough doesn't get droopy while you fuss over your berry slices.

For this tart, use very small strawberries, halved. If yours are larger, quarter or slice them. You may need to carefully deflate the tart shell as it bakes; if you see a puff beginning, first attempt to deflate it by carefully lifting up the crust, near the offending bubble, with your offset spatula, and then, if that doesn't have any effect, even more carefully poke a hole with your paring knife, just deep enough into the dough to release the air, being sure not to go all the way through to the bottom of the crust. You may need to hover over your tart for a few minutes, lifting or stabbing, but once the crust sets, you can ignore it and leave it to bake in peace.

1. On a lightly floured work surface, with a lightly floured rolling pin, roll the tart dough to a 12-inch (30.5-centimeter) circle, then roll the outer ¾ inch (2 centimeters) of the circle a little thinner, until the dough is 13 inches (33 centimeters) in diameter. Transfer to a parchment-lined cookie sheet or round pizza pan big enough to hold the tart and refrigerate until very firm, about 45 minutes.

2. Arrange an oven rack in the bottom third of the oven, place a pizza stone on it, if using, and preheat the oven to 425°F (220°C).

3. **MAKE THE FILLING:** In a small bowl, combine the crumbs and flour. Remove the chilled dough from the refrigerator and, with an offset spatula, spread the almond cream all over the dough, leaving a ½-inch (1.5-centimeter) border. Sprinkle the crumb-flour mixture over evenly and pat gently so it sticks to the almond cream. Fold the border of the tart over, twisting it loosely under itself to form a rope-shaped edge. Return the dough to the refrigerator while you prepare the berries.

(continued)

APRICOT-CHERRY COBBLER

Serves 6

FOR THE BISCUITS

1½ cups (180 grams) all-purpose flour, plus more for dusting

¾ cup (90 grams) cake or pastry flour

3 tablespoons (36 grams) granulated sugar

2 teaspoons baking powder

½ teaspoon kosher salt

6 tablespoons (85 grams) cold unsalted butter, cubed, plus more for greasing the baking dish

1 cup (237 milliliters) heavy cream

1½ tablespoons (21 grams) unsalted butter, melted

1½ tablespoons Demerara sugar (see page 21), for sprinkling

FOR THE FRUIT

2½ pounds (1.36 kilograms) apricots, halved, pitted, and cut into ½-inch (1.5-centimeter) wedges

2 cups (340 grams) cherries, stemmed, pitted, and halved

½ to ¾ cup (99 to 150 grams) granulated sugar (please taste!)

3 to 4 teaspoons tapioca flour (see page 21)

Cold (unwhipped) compound cream (see pages 330–337) for serving (optional)

Fruit cobblers are my favorite manifestation of cooked summer fruits. You don't need to add spice to the fruit; let the ripeness express itself in taste and aroma. Cobblers are best served warm, in bowls, with a pitcher of cold infused heavy cream (see the chapter on compound creams, page 326); if unwhipped, these are pourable). The combination of tart apricots and sweet cherries, which come into season at the same time where I am in California, is just one suggestion; nectarines and raspberries also pair well, as do peaches and blueberries. In fact, most other juicy summer fruits, either solo or in concert, would be good.

1. **MAKE THE BISCUITS:** Preheat the oven to 375°F (190°C).

2. In a bowl, whisk together the flours, granulated sugar, baking powder, and salt. Using a pastry blender or two butter knives, cut in the cold butter until it is the size of peas. Stir in the cream with a fork until a shaggy dough forms.

3. Turn the dough out onto a lightly floured surface and knead two or three times, just until it comes together. Roll into a 9-inch (23-centimeter) round about ½ inch (1.5 centimeters) thick. Using a 3-inch (8-centimeter) biscuit cutter, cut out 5 biscuits. Gently gather the scraps together, reroll them, and cut out one more round, for a total of 6 biscuits. Transfer the biscuits to a baking sheet, brush with the melted butter, and sprinkle the tops with Demerara sugar, then transfer the biscuits to the refrigerator while you prepare the fruit.

4. **BAKE THE FRUIT:** Butter a baking dish. The optimal vessel is wider than it is deep—think gratin dish, not soufflé mold. A 9-by-13-inch (23-by-33-centimeter) baking dish or similar works well. In a medium bowl, combine the apricots, cherries, ½ cup (99 grams) granulated sugar, and 1 tablespoon tapioca flour. Toss gently to coat and let stand for 5 minutes.

5. If your fruit seems especially juicy, stir in the remaining teaspoon of tapioca flour. If the fruit seems tart, add some (or all) of the remaining ¼ cup (50 grams) granulated sugar. Transfer to the prepared baking dish and bake just until the fruit juices begin to bubble at the edges of the pan, about 15 minutes.

(continued)

6. Remove the baking dish from the oven, gently stir the fruit, and give it a quick taste; you can add a little more granulated sugar right here if you didn't quite nail it. Lay the prepared biscuits on top of the hot fruit. Return to the oven and bake until the biscuits are golden brown and the fruit juices are thick and syrupy, 25 to 30 minutes longer. Let cool on a wire rack.

7. Serve warm or at room temperature, preferably with a drizzle of cold compound cream. The cobbler is best eaten the same day it's made, but it can be reheated in a 375°F (190°C) oven for 15 minutes with not too disappointing a result.

VARIATION

Any-Fruit Shortcake

These tender biscuits are brilliant companions to fruit that you want to eat raw, such as perfectly ripe, juicy berries or stone fruits (use about ¾ cup sliced or chopped fruit per shortcake), along with a simple (or compound) whipped cream. You'd have to go pretty far afield to mess this up, so spread your wings a little and invent your own combination. Here are some of my favorites.

> Strawberries with Lemon Verbena Cream (page 332)
>
> Nectarines or peaches with Rose Geranium Cream (page 331)
>
> Huckleberries, pears, or quinces with Meyer Lemon Cream (page 333)
>
> Apricots or cherries with Peach Leaf Cream (page 334)
>
> Blood oranges, tangerines, or Candied Kumquats (page 89) with Coconut Cream (page 336)

1. Preheat the oven to 375°F (190°C) and make the biscuits as described on the previous page. Place on a sheet pan, spacing them a few inches (about 8 centimeters) apart. Bake until golden brown, about 25 minutes.

2. In a medium bowl, combine the fruit with sugar to taste. Let macerate for 10 minutes while you prepare the whipped cream (plain or compound) of your choice (see pages 330–337).

3. To serve, split each biscuit open and spoon some of the fruit and its juices onto the bottom half of each one. Top with a spoonful of the whipped cream and the biscuit top. Serve right away. (Any leftover unfilled biscuits can be revived in the oven just like the cobbler; see step 7, opposite.)

STREUSELKUCHEN
(Viennese Coffee Cake with Raspberries)

Makes one 9-inch (23-centimeter) cake; serves 10 to 12

FOR THE DOUGH

3½ cups (400 grams) all-purpose flour

¼ cup (50 grams) granulated sugar

1½ teaspoons kosher salt

1½ teaspoons freshly grated nutmeg

¾ teaspoon baking powder

½ pound (224 grams) cold unsalted butter, cut into slices ⅛ inch (0.3 centimeter) thick, plus more for greasing the pan

3 tablespoons (30 grams) crumbled fresh (cake) yeast or 1 tablespoon plus 1 teaspoon (12 grams) instant dry yeast

⅔ cup (140 milliliters) whole milk

1 large egg

3 large egg yolks

FOR THE STREUSEL

1⅔ cups (200 grams) all-purpose flour

¾ cup (96 grams) hazelnuts, lightly toasted and cooled

⅔ cup (130 grams) light Muscovado sugar

1 teaspoon kosher salt

(continued)

The dough for this cake is both unbelievably resilient and versatile. You can roll it for cinnamon buns, load it with butter and huckleberries and bake it in muffin cups, or fill it with hazelnuts, orange marmalade, and chocolate and bake it in a kugelhopf mold. In other words, it's a kitchen MVP, with countless uses. Of all the things you can make with the dough, though, this simple coffee cake is my favorite. You can use any ripe berries, but raspberries are particularly good. Note that the dough needs to rest overnight, so plan accordingly.

1. **MAKE THE DOUGH:** In a large bowl, whisk together the flour, granulated sugar, salt, nutmeg, and baking powder. With a pastry blender, two knives, or your fingers, cut the butter into the dry ingredients until the pieces of butter are the size of chickpeas. Make a well in the center of the dry ingredients.

2. In a small bowl, whisk together the yeast, milk, egg, and egg yolks. Pour the wet ingredients into the well in the dry ingredients and, using your hand like a claw, rake the dry ingredients into the wet and mix until combined. Turn out onto a floured work surface and knead once or twice to finish combining the ingredients.

3. Wrap the dough tightly in plastic wrap and refrigerate overnight. (*At this point the dough can be frozen for up to a month; let thaw overnight in the refrigerator before using.*)

4. **MAKE THE STREUSEL:** Combine the flour and nuts in the bowl of a food processor and process until the nuts are finely ground. Add the Muscovado sugar, salt, cinnamon, and mace and process until combined. Turn out into a bowl.

5. Drizzle the melted butter over the dry mixture, using your hand as a claw, and rake together until little split pea–size clumps form (think Hostess crumb cakes). Spread out on a quarter sheet pan and refrigerate for 20 minutes.

6. With your fingers, rake through and separate the clumps of streusel again, then transfer to a lidded container and store in the refrigerator or

facedown in the pan (the part next to the pit is what you want to see while you're arranging the fruit, not the pretty part of the skin). Set aside to cool to room temp while you make the cake batter.

4. **MAKE THE CAKE:** Sift the flour, baking powder, and baking soda into a medium bowl. In the bowl of a stand mixer fitted with the paddle attachment (or in a large bowl, using a handheld mixer), cream the butter, sugar, and salt on medium-high speed until light and fluffy, about 5 minutes. Reduce the speed to low and add the eggs one at a time, beating after each addition until the batter looks emulsified. Add the dry ingredients in 3 additions, alternating with the buttermilk (if you're making this with a handheld mixer, stir in the dry ingredients, alternating with the buttermilk, by hand). Continue mixing (or stirring) until the batter is smooth.

5. Transfer the cake batter to the prepared pan and use an offset spatula to smooth the top. Bake until the cake is deep golden brown and springs back when touched, 55 minutes to 1 hour. Transfer to a wire rack and let the cake cool in the pan for 10 minutes.

6. Run a small offset spatula, with the front of it facing outward, around the edges of the cake, pressing the spatula against the pan so you don't cut into the cake. Invert a serving plate over the cake pan and turn the cake out onto the plate. Carefully remove the pan. Let the cake cool completely before serving. (*Or, if you are making the cake ahead, let it cool completely in the pan, then refrigerate, still in the pan, for up to 2 days. When you're ready to serve, warm the cake in a low oven, then set the pan on a low burner for about 30 seconds to make sure the caramel melts and invert it.*)

7. Cut the cake into wedges and serve.

PLUM KUCHEN

Makes one 9-by-13-inch (23-by-33-centimeter) tart; serves 10 to 12

FOR THE DOUGH

5 tablespoons (71 grams) unsalted butter, melted and cooled

3 tablespoons (36 grams) sugar

½ teaspoon kosher salt

5 tablespoons (71 grams) unsalted butter, very soft

1½ cups (180 grams) all-purpose flour, sifted

1 tablespoon poppy seeds (see page 20)

FOR THE FILLING AND GLAZE

7 medium firm-ripe plums (about 1 pound/454 grams)

4 large egg whites

½ teaspoon cream of tartar

¼ cup plus 2 tablespoons (72 grams) sugar

1 teaspoon tapioca flour (see page 21)

½ cup (113 grams) Almond Cream (page 43), at room temperature

Café Sperl is a traditional Viennese cafe. It is not like Café Central (the grandest of the cafes in Vienna), but it has a beautiful faded glory. Their kuchen is the first thing I tried to replicate when I returned home from my first visit to central Europe. According to the *Ober* (waiter), the plums they use at Sperl have been sourced from the same grower for twenty years.

This kuchen is more like a tart than a cake. The poppy seed short crust is topped with a layer of meringue-lightened almond cream, and thin plum wedges are meticulously arranged on top. When the kuchen is baked, the plums turn dark and glossy while the meringue puffs up around them, creating a cakey layer with a crusty top. The short crust is made with an unusual method; instead of using all melted butter, as is the case with many shortbread recipes, it uses half melted butter and half very soft butter, which makes the crust unbelievably tender but with more structure than one made entirely with soft butter. Make sure your melted butter has cooled before you add the soft butter, or it will *all* become melted!

1. **MAKE THE DOUGH:** In a medium bowl, whisk together the cooled melted butter, the sugar, and salt. Whisk in the soft butter. Switch to a rubber spatula and stir in the flour and poppy seeds, mixing until just incorporated.

2. Using a quarter sheet pan as a guide, trace a 9-by-13-inch (23-by-33-centimeter) rectangle in the center of a 12-by-17-inch (30.5-by-44-centimeter) sheet of parchment with a dark marker. Flip the parchment over; you should be able to see the lines through the paper. Transfer the dough to the center of the rectangle and use a small offset spatula to spread it into an even layer. Top with a second sheet of parchment, then use a rolling pin to roll the dough out to the size of the rectangle you drew and level out the dough. If the dough spreads beyond the border of the rectangle, use the edge of your offset spatula to scootch it back within the rectangle's border. Remove the top sheet of parchment.

3. Trim the long sides of the parchment flush with the dough and then press the dough (still on the parchment) into a quarter sheet pan. Trim the shorter sides of the paper so there is a slight overhang beyond the edges of the pan (these will be your handles when removing the kuchen). Refrigerate for at least 30 minutes, or up to overnight. (*The dough can be wrapped well and frozen at this point.*)

(continued)

4. Preheat the oven to 300°F (150°C).

5. Remove the sheet pan from the refrigerator and transfer to the oven. Bake the crust for 15 minutes, then reduce the oven temperature to 250°F (120°C). Use the palm of your hand to gently pat down any bubbles that may have begun to form. Continue baking until the crust is dark golden brown, 10 to 15 minutes longer. Transfer to a wire rack and let cool slightly. Increase the oven temperature to 350°F (175°C).

6. MAKE THE FILLING: Halve 6 of the plums, remove the pits, and slice each half into thin wedges, 5 or 6 pieces per half. Set aside.

7. In the bowl of a stand mixer fitted with the whisk attachment (or in a large bowl, using a handheld mixer), beat the egg whites on low speed until foamy. Add the cream of tartar, increase the speed to medium-high, and gradually add 2 tablespoons (24 grams) of the sugar. Continue beating until the egg whites hold stiff peaks, then beat in the tapioca flour.

8. Put the almond cream in a large bowl and stir in about one-third of the beaten egg whites to lighten the mixture, then fold in the remaining egg whites until no white streaks remain. Spread the almond cream mixture over the baked dough in an even layer, spreading it all the way to the edges. Arrange the plum wedges in rows on top of the almond cream, shingling the slices slightly, until the entire tart is covered. Sprinkle the top with 2 tablespoons (24 grams) sugar.

9. Transfer the tart to the oven and bake until lightly browned and set, 25 to 30 minutes. Let cool on a wire rack.

10. WHILE THE TART BAKES, MAKE THE GLAZE: Pit and chop the remaining plum and place in a saucepan with the remaining 2 tablespoons (24 grams) sugar and enough water to cover—about 3 tablespoons (45 milliliters). Bring to a boil and cook, pressing on the plum pieces, until the fruit is soft and the liquid is syrupy, about 10 minutes. Strain through a fine-mesh sieve (save the fruit—it's great stirred into yogurt). Brush the glaze over the top of the tart while it's still warm.

11. To serve, cut the tart into rectangular slices, doing your best to avoid cutting through the nicely sliced fruit, and serve warm or at room temperature. This tart is best eaten the same day it's baked.

HUCKLEBERRY-PECAN UPSIDE-DOWN CAKE

Makes one 9-inch (23-centimeter) cake; serves 10 to 12

FOR THE CARAMEL

1 cup (170 grams) sugar

8 tablespoons (113 grams) unsalted butter

2 cups (340 grams) huckleberries

FOR THE CAKE

1 cup plus 3 tablespoons (142 grams) all-purpose flour

1 cup (125 grams) pecans, toasted and cooled

1½ teaspoons baking powder

½ teaspoon baking soda

¾ cup plus 3 tablespoons (222 milliliters) buttermilk

1 teaspoon vanilla extract

12 tablespoons (170 grams) unsalted butter, at room temperature

1 cup plus 2 tablespoons (216 grams) sugar

¼ teaspoon plus ⅛ teaspoon kosher salt

3 large eggs

Whipped Cream (page 330) or ice cream for serving (optional)

Huckleberries are wonderfully tart, a little earthy, and wild and gamey all at once, pairing beautifully with pecans. If you can't find huckleberries, you can substitute another tart wild berry, or even fresh sour cherries. This cake is similar to the Ginger-Plum Upside-Down Cake (page 51), but with a portion of the flour replaced by ground pecans, which gives it a sweet, toasty flavor. This cake is equally good for dessert or breakfast (with or without a generous spoonful of whipped cream).

1. Preheat the oven to 350°F (175°C). Have a 9-inch (23-centimeter) round cake pan ready.

2. **MAKE THE CARAMEL:** Heat the sugar in a medium heavy-bottomed saucepan over medium-high heat. As the sugar begins to melt at the edges, use a heatproof spatula to pull the melted sugar into the center, then continue cooking, stirring occasionally, until the caramel is a deep reddish-amber color and beginning to smoke. If at any point it looks grainy or clumpy, reduce the heat to low and cook, stirring, until smooth. When the caramel is ready, remove the pan from the heat and whisk in the butter; the mixture will foam vigorously. Pour the caramel into the cake pan, tilting the pan so the caramel covers the entire bottom. Arrange the berries in an even layer in the caramel while it is still hot, then let cool.

3. **MAKE THE CAKE:** In the bowl of a food processor, combine the flour and pecans and process until the nuts are finely ground. Transfer to a bowl and whisk in the baking powder and baking soda. Combine the buttermilk and vanilla in a measuring cup.

4. In the bowl of a stand mixer fitted with the paddle attachment (or in a large bowl, using a handheld mixer), cream the butter, sugar, and salt on medium-high speed until light and fluffy, about 4 minutes. Reduce the speed to low and add the eggs one at a time, beating after each addition. Add the dry ingredients in 3 additions, alternating with the buttermilk (if you're making this with a handheld mixer, stir in the dry ingredients, alternating with the buttermilk, by hand), mixing until the batter is smooth.

5. Transfer the cake batter to the prepared pan and use an offset spatula to smooth the top. Bake until the cake is deep golden brown and the top

springs back when touched, 55 minutes to 1 hour. Transfer to a wire rack and let the cake cool in the pan for 10 minutes.

6. Run a small offset spatula, with the front of it facing outward, around the edges of the cake, pressing the spatula against the pan so you don't cut into the cake. Invert a serving plate over the cake pan and turn the cake out onto the plate. Carefully remove the pan. Let cool completely before serving. (*Or, if you are making the cake ahead, let it cool completely in the pan, then refrigerate, still in the pan, for up to 2 days. When you're ready to serve, warm the cake in a low oven, then set the pan on a low burner for about 30 seconds to make sure the caramel melts and invert it.*)

7. Cut the cake into wedges and serve with whipped cream or Chicory Ice Cream (page 184), if desired.

HOT DATE TURNOVERS

Makes 12 turnovers

FOR THE DOUGH

1¾ cups plus 2 tablespoons (226 grams) all-purpose flour

½ teaspoon kosher salt

½ teaspoon sugar

½ pound (224 grams) cold unsalted butter, cut into 16 pats

1½ to 3 tablespoons (22 to 45 milliliters) ice water

FOR THE WALNUT FRANGIPANE

Scant ½ cup (55 grams) walnuts, toasted and cooled

1 tablespoon sugar

⅛ teaspoon kosher salt

1 large egg

1 tablespoon (14 grams) unsalted butter, soft but still cool

2 teaspoons grated orange zest

24 small dates, such as Barhi or Deglet Noor, or 12 large dates, such as Medjool (see page 18)

12 bite-size pieces toffee (one per turnover), homemade (page 235) or store-bought

TO FINISH

1 large egg, beaten, for egg wash

2 tablespoons (28 grams) unsalted butter, melted

1½ teaspoons sugar

(continued)

My mind was blown the first time I tasted a perfectly ripe Barhi date. Soft, creamy, and sweet, of course, but also complex, revealing notes of toffee, coffee, and orange, it inspired these little turnovers. But this flavor combination complements any variety of date, including the easier-to-find Medjool.

The dates are pitted and stuffed with bits of toffee, then tucked inside rounds of flaky pastry that has been smeared with orange zest–scented walnut frangipane. You can make your own toffee (see page 235) or fast-track these turnovers with store-bought toffee. Serve them warm, with Toffee Sauce (page 339), Candied Kumquats (page 89), and a spoonful of Crème Fraîche (page 337), and you've got a date so hot you'll want to marry it.

1. **MAKE THE DOUGH:** In a large bowl, combine the flour, salt, and sugar. Add half of the butter pats and, with a pastry cutter or your fingertips, work the butter into the dough until it is in pea-size pieces. Add the remaining pats of butter and work them into the dough until they're about half their original size. Slowly add the water, beginning with 1½ tablespoons and adding up to an additional 1½ tablespoons as needed. The dough will be very shaggy, with some dry spots; it will not come together into a homogeneous ball, and that is okay. Alternatively, you can make the dough in a stand mixer fitted with the paddle attachment (or in a large bowl, using a handheld mixer).

2. Turn the dough out onto a work surface and shape into a rough rectangle. Using the heel of your hand, press small amounts of the dough down and away from you in a firm smear about 6 inches (15 centimeters) long (this process is called fraisage, and it smears the butter into long tongues). Stack the tongues of pastry on top of one another as you go; when you're finished, you'll have a shaggy rectangular stack. With a rolling pin, gently roll over the stack to compact it into a tidier rectangle, then wrap in plastic wrap and refrigerate for 30 minutes.

3. Remove the dough from the refrigerator and, on a lightly floured work surface, with a lightly floured rolling pin, roll it into a rectangle that is 13 by 23 inches (33 by 58 centimeters), with a short end toward you. Use a dry pastry brush to brush off any excess flour. Cut the dough crosswise into three 8-by-13-inch (20-by-33-centimeter) rectangles, meticulously brushing off the excess flour. Stack the rectangles of dough on top of one

another, then turn the stack so a short side is in front of your belly. This is the first "turn." Roll the dough to an 8-by-18-inch (20-by-45-centimeter) rectangle, cover and chill for 30 to 45 minutes, until cold and firm.

4. Repeat the rolling, cutting, stacking, and chilling process two more times, for a total of 3 turns, resting the dough after each turn. After the third turn, chill the dough thoroughly before rolling out and cutting.

5. **WHILE THE DOUGH CHILLS, PREPARE THE WALNUT FRANGIPANE:** In a food processor, grind the nuts with the sugar and salt until fine. When the mixture just begins to clump up, add the egg and then the soft butter, processing until nice and creamy. Transfer the frangipane to a bowl and stir in the orange zest. Chill for 10 minutes before using. (*The walnut frangipane will keep for up to 1 month, stored in the refrigerator in an airtight container; bring to cool room temperature before using. The frangipane can also be frozen for up to 3 months; let come to cool room temperature before using.*)

6. Put the dates in a large bowl and add enough nearly boiling water to cover if using firm dates like Medjools, or room-temperature water if using soft dates like Barhis. Let stand for a few minutes, then, one at a time, remove the dates from the water and, with a sharp paring knife, peel them (the hot water softens and loosens the skins, so this is less tedious than it may sound, and some of the skin will come off without needing the knife), replenishing the water as needed. Set the dates on a paper towel–lined plate to drain.

7. Trim the hard blossom end off each date, then make a slit in one side of the date and pull out the pit. Fill the cavity of each date with a piece of toffee. If using small dates, you will need to squish pairs of them together, forming little "footballs." Set aside. (*The dates can be peeled and filled up to a day in advance; cover with plastic wrap and store in the refrigerator until you're ready to form the turnovers.*)

8. On a lightly floured work surface, with a lightly floured rolling pin, roll the dough into a rectangle measuring about 11 by 17 inches (28 by 44 centimeters). Transfer to a sheet of parchment, set on a sheet pan, and refrigerate until firm but not hard, about 15 minutes.

9. Remove the chilled dough from the refrigerator. Using a 4-inch (10-centimeter) round cutter, stamp out 12 rounds and set on a sheet of parchment.

10. Working with one round of dough at a time, place 1 teaspoon of walnut frangipane in the center of the round and, with a small offset spatula, spread it into a thin, even circle, leaving a ¼-inch (0.5-centimeter) border all around. Set 1 large filled date or 1 date football in the center, then brush the exposed edges of the dough with some of the egg wash. Fold the dough over the filling, forming a half-moon, and press hard to seal. Set on a parchment-lined sheet pan and refrigerate for 15 minutes.

11. Preheat the oven to 375°F (190°C).

12. Remove the turnovers from the fridge and, using your thumb and index finger, pinch a pretty ruffle into the sealed edges of each turnover. Pinch hard, like you're mad at it, to crimp it and seal it really well (otherwise, it may come unsealed in the oven). Return the pinched turnovers to the baking sheet, spacing them evenly. Brush each with melted butter, then sprinkle with a fairy dusting of sugar. With the tip of a sharp knife, cut 3 little steam vents close to the folded side of each turnover (they should resemble chicken feet). (*The unbaked turnovers can be frozen at this point; freeze on a parchment-lined sheet pan in a single layer, then transfer to a plastic freezer bag and freeze for up to 1 month. Bake from frozen, adding 2 minutes to the baking time.*)

13. Transfer the turnovers to the oven and bake until golden brown, 23 to 25 minutes. Transfer to a wire rack and let cool slightly. The turnovers are best served warm (but not so hot that you will burn your mouth) and best eaten the same day they are made.

CRANBERRY-GINGER UPSIDE-DOWN CAKES

Makes 8 to 12 individual cakes, depending on the ramekins you use

FOR THE CARAMEL

½ cup (99 grams) sugar

4 tablespoons (57 grams) unsalted butter

2 cups (210 grams) fresh cranberries

FOR THE CAKE

½ cup (99 grams) sugar

½ cup (118 milliliters) grapeseed or vegetable oil

¾ cup plus 3 tablespoons (222 milliliters) blackstrap molasses

1 tablespoon honey

½ cup (118 milliliters) boiling water

1 teaspoon baking soda

One 2½-ounce (71-gram) piece fresh ginger, peeled and grated (about ¼ cup)

1¼ cups (150 grams) all-purpose flour

¼ teaspoon ground cloves

¼ teaspoon ground cinnamon

1 large egg, beaten

Meyer Lemon Cream (page 333) for serving (optional)

These cakes have a warming, homey quality that fits perfectly into the Christmas season. With lots of spice from fresh ginger, bitterness from blackstrap molasses, and brightness from tart cranberries, the cakes produce a smell while baking that will surely put you in the holiday spirit (even if you're like me and can't have a Christmas tree because your crazy cats will break all of your antique ornaments). Just the batter baked on its own—without its cranberry-caramel topper—makes a damn fine cake, and it's practically healthy with the good amount of iron from the molasses.

Be sure that all the cranberries have popped and deflated before you pour the batter over them; if they are not fully popped, the berries will lift from the bed of caramel, up and into the cake. Serve with Meyer Lemon Cream (page 333), if you like.

1. Preheat the oven to 350°F (175°C). Butter eight 8-ounce (237-milliliter) or twelve 6-ounce (178-milliliter) ramekins.

2. **MAKE THE CARAMEL:** Heat the sugar in a medium heavy-bottomed saucepan over medium-high heat. As the sugar begins to melt at the edges, use a heatproof spatula to pull the melted sugar into the center, then continue cooking, stirring occasionally, until the caramel is a deep reddish-amber color. If at any point it looks grainy or clumpy, reduce the heat to low and cook, stirring, until smooth. Remove the pan from the heat and whisk in the butter; the mixture will foam vigorously.

3. Divide the caramel among the ramekins, then top with the cranberries. Set the ramekins on a sheet pan and transfer to the oven. Bake for 10 minutes, or until the cranberries are popped and deflated. Remove from the oven and stab the cranberries with a fork to ensure that they're fully popped. Return the ramekins to the oven and bake for 5 minutes longer. Remove from the oven and let the ramekins and caramel cool completely before proceeding. (You can pop the ramekins into the fridge to speed the process, or even do this step a day ahead.)

4. **MAKE THE CAKE:** In a large bowl, stir together the sugar, oil, molasses, and honey. Combine the boiling water and baking soda in a measuring cup, then pour into the sugar mixture and stir to combine. Stir in the ginger. In a separate bowl, whisk together the flour, cloves, and cinnamon, then

VARIATION

If you want to make it fancy, bake the cake in individual ramekins, in the water bath, until the tops start to brown and the cakes are beginning to pull away from the sides, about 30 minutes. A half recipe will yield enough batter for six 6-ounce (178-milliliter) ramekins or four 8-ounce (237-milliliter) ones. Serve the cakes warm from the oven, or rewarm in a 350°F (175°C) oven before serving. Loosen the sides of the cakes with a baby offset spatula, unmold onto serving plates, and garnish the top (formerly the bottom) of each one with a slice of Candied Meyer Lemon (page 87), if you like. Serve with sliced strawberries or citrus supremes and Coconut Cream (page 336) or Rose Geranium Cream (page 331) if you really want to stop the show!

TANGERINE AND COFFEE GRANITA

Serves 8

FOR THE TANGERINE GRANITA

2 cups (473 milliliters) freshly squeezed tangerine juice (from about 12 juicy tangerines)

¼ cup (50 grams) sugar

Pinch of kosher salt

FOR THE COFFEE GRANITA

2 cups (473 milliliters) cold coffee (see the New Orleans Iced-Coffee Float, page 185, for a great iced coffee recipe)

¼ cup (50 grams) sugar

Pinch of kosher salt

Coconut-Caramel Ice Cream (see page 190)

½ cup (87 grams) pomegranate seeds for garnish (optional but magical)

Even though granita is so easy to make, it can be tough to find a good one. The key to this semi-frozen dessert is to stir the granita as soon as the first ice crystals form, to set a very open texture, and then, once these flakes are frozen—but not rock hard—to scrape them with a fork into delicate snow. If you forget about the granita and it has frozen solid, be sure to let it defrost a little before scraping, or instead of flakes, you will get chunks. Delicious chunks, but still—not the desired effect. If you don't want to make the coconut-caramel ice cream I like to serve with these granitas, they are spectacular on their own, or you can drizzle mounded scoops of granita with a bit of full-fat coconut milk for a ritzy snow cone.

1. **MAKE THE TANGERINE GRANITA:** In a bowl, stir together the tangerine juice, sugar, and salt until the sugar dissolves.

2. **MAKE THE COFFEE GRANITA:** In a bowl, stir together the coffee, sugar, and salt until the sugar dissolves.

3. Pour the tangerine mixture and coffee mixture into two separate freezer-proof vessels; the liquid should be at least ½ inch (1.5 centimeters) but no more than 1 inch (2.5 centimeters) deep; loaf pans work well. Transfer to the freezer and freeze until just set; the mixtures should be a little slushy but not hard (about 1 hour).

4. Remove the pans from the freezer and whisk each granita; you want to separate, not demolish, the ice crystals that have formed. Return the pans to the freezer. Freeze until firm but not rock hard, about 45 minutes.

5. Remove from the freezer and, with a fork, scrape each pan of granita, making beautiful flakes of flavored ice. Return to the freezer. (*The granitas will keep for several days; fluff with a fork before serving.*)

6. When it's time to serve, fluff the granitas with a fork. (Make sure the granita is not a hard block when you do this, or you'll ruin the texture—if it's solidly frozen, let it stand at room temperature until it is slightly softened but before it starts to slushify, and fluff again with a fork.)

7. To serve, scoop some of the coconut-caramel ice cream into each of six coupes and top with a scoop each of the tangerine and coffee granita. Garnish with the pomegranate seeds.

PRESERVES

Do you ever wonder why we are so fascinated by traditional methods of canning, dehydrating, and lacto-fermenting? When agricultural science and modern shipping have almost eliminated the need to preserve, why do we persevere in upholding these traditions? I think it's because we create a connection to the past, near and far, when we preserve. Whether it's canning an heirloom variety of plum from our best-loved farmer to use in an annual Christmas pudding, re-creating the fruit filling for a cookie that was a favorite of an Austro-Hungarian prince, or preserving a bumper crop from your backyard to give as gifts, there is a feeling of connectedness to other cooks and bakers, across time and space, when you put up fruit. Then there are the practical reasons: Preserving is a wonderful way to concentrate flavor, capture fruit at its absolute peak, and bring about a miraculous change in its texture and flavor.

From left to right: Apricot Jam (page 78); Faux Red Currant Jam (page 86); Super-Speedy, but a Little Seedy, Raspberry Jam (page 83); Kumquat Marmalade (page 88); Damson Plum Preserves (page 80); Sour Orange Marmalade (page 84)

Preserves also play a central role, in both their flavor and their composition, in the traditional cakes and pastries of old Europe: A Sacher torte is not a Sacher torte without apricot preserves, and what is a linzer torte without the jam?

There is a science to making perfect jams, jellies, and preserves, but I leave science to the scientists and preserve with a mind that is equal parts pastry chef and grandma. When preserving, I look for what I want in all my fruit desserts: balance, texture, and a pure expression of fruit. I definitely have some tricks, though, which I will share with you. Each of these preserves uses a slightly different technique, which you can apply to similar fruits. Most of the recipes in this section are used as components of another dessert, but that is not to say the preserves can't be smeared on toast or bottled and tied with a bow and gifted to some worthy recipient.

TRADITIONAL AND MOSTLY TRADITIONAL CAKES AND TORTES

When I embarked on my first journey to central Europe—specifically, Austria, Hungary, the Czech Republic, and Croatia—I was not looking for ideas for a future restaurant, nor was I planning to become singularly obsessed with a part of the world or a cuisine. I merely planned to do a little time travel, show off my best outfits, and eat many, many cakes. Which I did. But when I returned to the States, I realized that a seed had been planted, and that the trip set me on the path to opening my San Francisco restaurant, 20th Century Cafe.

The cakes and tortes in this chapter are a glimpse into the world you enter when you pass through the doorway of a *Konditorei*, or pastry shop, in Vienna. What makes a torte a torte and a cake a cake, you say? Some say a torte is a cake composed of many thin layers, usually with little or no flour in the batter, often made with nuts, and filled with jam, buttercream, or chocolate. Some say a torte must be round, and some say a torte is just a fancy name for a cake!

These recipes are definitely fancy cakes. Even the ones for cheesecakes, with crusts that are baked separately from the soft, creamy cake, turn this ubiquitous dessert into something quite special. Many of the recipes in this chapter, including the Sacher Torte, Linzer Torte, and Dobos Torta, are my versions of very traditional pastries, while others, such as the Kókusz Torta and Date-Pistachio Torte, are perhaps not traditional but are very much in the spirit of central European desserts. These are beautiful, exacting, elegant desserts that rely on both good technique and good ingredients, but they reward you for your efforts. Most of the layered cakes keep well, so you can make them even a day ahead. In fact, some, like the Dobos Torta and the Esterházy Schnitten, are better the second day, and the Honey Cake absolutely requires an overnight rest in the fridge before serving.

The cakes in this chapter are made by hand, with little machinery and with meticulous care. Since these recipes can be pretty time-consuming, I've broken down the steps wherever possible, so that you can make them even if you don't have several hours in one day to dedicate to a cake-making project. Please don't be intimidated by them. Every cake in this chapter is well worth all of your time and effort, not just for the pleasure of baking, and the pride you'll feel when you succeed, or the accolades you may tire of hearing from those lucky enough to taste your creations. When you get to eat something this good that you made yourself, you will know, in your own heart, that you truly are an advanced baker.

Skills and Equipment

As you work through this chapter, you will build on skills first presented in the fruit chapter, including making meringue, folding, and spreading batters like a master. There are a few simple and inexpensive pieces of equipment that are critical to making these cakes: a small offset spatula, two quarter sheet pans, two half sheet pans (just referred to as sheet pans here, as a whole sheet pan wouldn't fit into a home oven), a fluted tart pan with a removable bottom, a large metal bowl, and a large rubber spatula (that nobody in the house is allowed to use for savory projects) for folding. For recipes that call for beaten egg whites (of which there are many), you can use a stand mixer (easiest), a handheld mixer (less easy), or a whisk and a copper bowl (good for arm muscles and bragging rights). Note that if you choose to use a copper bowl, you should omit the cream of tartar from the recipe; not only would it be redundant, but the tartaric acid would actually pull some copper into the mixture, and eating that is a big fat no-no. Other than these few tools, you can improvise almost anything else!

Back row, from left to right: Walnut-Apricot Torte (page 117), Flódni (page 145), Dobos Torta (page 131), Honey Cake (page 151); Front row, from left to right: Esterházy Schnitten (page 125), Cecil Cannon's Favorite Meyer Lemon–Coconut Cheesecake (page 105), Date-Pistachio Torte (page 123), Chestnut-Apple Linzer Torte (page 141), Kókusz Torta (page 109)

MOHNKUCHEN
(Poppy Seed Cake with Jam Filling)

*Makes 1 rectangular cake;
serves 6 to 8*

FOR THE CAKE

6 tablespoons (85 grams) unsalted butter, at room temperature, plus more for greasing the pan

1 cup (156 grams) poppy seeds (see page 20)

⅔ cup less 1 teaspoon (133 grams) granulated sugar

½ teaspoon kosher salt

4 large eggs, separated, at room temperature

Pinch of cream of tartar

¾ teaspoon tapioca flour (see page 21)

FOR ASSEMBLY

1 recipe Sour Cherry Lekvar (page 38) or ¾ cup (178 milliliters) Faux Red Currant Jam (page 86)

Confectioners' sugar for dusting

Whipped Cream (page 330) for serving

This jammy poppy seed cake was inspired by a request for a dessert appropriate for Passover—I pored over my books and racked my brain to come up with some new flourless desserts for the holiday, and this cake was born.

The "flour" in this cake—called Mohnkuchen in German and makos torta in Hungarian—is actually ground poppy seeds. Here's the kicker: After developing this Passover-appropriate flourless dessert, I learned that poppy seeds are *kitniyot* (a collective term for foods that are forbidden for Ashkenazi Jews to eat on Passover), and most Jews in America do not consume *kitniyot* at Passover. I guess the rest of us can be the benefactors of my cultural snafu.

1. **MAKE THE CAKE:** Preheat the oven to 350°F (175°C). Lightly butter a quarter sheet pan and line with parchment.

2. Grind the poppy seeds in a blender or in batches in a spice grinder until they resemble clumpy, moist soil (see How—and How Not—to Grind Poppy Seeds, page 99).

3. In the bowl of a stand mixer fitted with the paddle attachment (or in a large bowl, with a handheld mixer), cream the butter, ⅓ cup (66 grams) of the granulated sugar, and the salt on medium speed until light and fluffy, about 4 minutes. Reduce the speed to low, add the ground poppy seeds, and mix to combine, then scrape down the sides of the bowl with a rubber spatula. Add the egg yolks and mix to combine. Transfer to a large bowl and wash and dry the mixer bowl (if using a stand mixer).

4. Switch to the whisk attachment, add the egg whites to the clean mixer bowl (or another large bowl if using a handheld mixer), and beat the egg whites on low speed until foamy. Add the cream of tartar, increase the speed to medium-high, and gradually begin adding the remaining ⅓ cup (66 grams) granulated sugar. Then continue whipping until the whites hold firm peaks. Add the tapioca flour and whip for another 15 seconds to combine. Remove the bowl (if using a stand mixer) and fold one-third of the beaten whites into the poppy seed mixture to lighten it. Then fold in the remaining whites in 2 additions, folding until no white streaks remain (See Eggs 101, page 100).

(continued)

Traditional and Mostly Traditional Cakes and Tortes　97

Eggs 101

EGGS ARE MAGICAL; they have superpowers, and this chapter would be nothing without them. I use large eggs in these recipes. But if you use extra-large, the recipes will still be okay—nothing here is that fussy. What *are* fussy are my techniques for whipping and folding egg whites. The first of these is pretty standard, but let's review it anyway.

Make sure your bowl and beater (and the hands that separate your eggs) are clean, clean, clean. I always rewash my bowl and whip before beating. I used to be religious about using warm egg whites, but I've gotten away with cold ones so often that I've abandoned this as a core belief. Call me a heretic!

When making a meringue, start the egg whites on low speed. When the eggs are foamy, increase the speed slightly and add the cream of tartar, unless you are using a copper bowl. (If you are, do not use cream of tartar, lemon juice, or anything other than sugar to stabilize your egg foam! The acid will pull an unhealthy amount of copper into the ingredients, so you don't want to do this—ever.) Once the foam starts becoming opaque and denser, slowly add the sugar. Adding the sugar too soon will weigh down the whites, preventing the foam from reaching maximum volume, and adding it too late will give you a less stable foam, which means your bubbles will burst instead of expanding beautifully. Keeping all of this in mind, I've had my bathroom ceiling spring a leak mid-meringue, and the cake still came out fine, so don't get too neurotic; just be careful (put a bucket under the leak and tell the family to chill out while you finish the cake).

Each recipe indicates the desired consistency of the egg foam; to check, give the meringue a stir with the whisk you've been using (be that the mixer attachment or a balloon whisk). Gently lift it out of the bowl and turn it upright. Look at it: Does the meringue curl? A little or a lot? Is it pointy? How pointy? This is what is meant by soft, medium, firm, or stiff peaks.

When the desired consistency is obtained, I use the whisk itself to introduce the egg foam into the base, rather than introduce the base into the foam, because sometimes the meringue will need a little more whisking, but once you introduce fat into the egg whites, that door is closed *forever*. I use the rubber spatula only for my final addition of egg whites.

As for actual folding, food scientist Harold McGee asserts that the velocity at which we fold an egg foam affects the loss in volume, so I always fold with a steady, even motion, turning the spatula in my hand as I complete each rotation, then introducing it sideways into the base, rather than flopping the mixture over, which does cause a noticeable reduction in volume over the course of the folding. It takes a while to get the hang of it, but once you do, you'll go nuts watching the way other people fold!

The final step of spreading the batter into the cake pan can be another volume-decreasing pitfall. Do it in such a way as to distribute the batter *over* the bottom of the pan, rather than just pour it all into the middle. The less you have to move the batter, the more volume it will retain. Spread very carefully with your offset spatula, focusing with all of your attention, only moving the batter as much as necessary and being sure to get those corners even. Then get the cake in the oven before it deflates!

4 tablespoons (57 grams)
unsalted butter, melted and
cooled

1 tablespoon beaten egg white

2 teaspoons granulated sugar
for sprinkling

4. **MAKE THE CRUST:** Preheat the oven to 275°F (133°C). Using a dark marker, draw a circle the size of the pan you are using on a sheet of parchment, then flip the paper over and place it on a sheet pan.

5. In a medium bowl, combine the coconut, confectioners' sugar, and salt. Stir in the butter and egg white until combined. Transfer to the center of the circle you traced and press into an even 10-inch (25-centimeter) or 9-inch (23-centimeter) round, depending on the size of the pan you're using to bake the cake.

6. Bake the crust until golden brown, 12 to 15 minutes, then transfer the pan to a wire rack and let cool completely. Once it is cool, carefully peel off the parchment.

7. **TO ASSEMBLE THE CHEESECAKE:** Remove the cheesecake from the refrigerator. Run a small offset spatula, with the front of it facing outward, around the edges of the cake, pressing against the pan so you don't cut into the cake. Then swirl the pan over a low burner to warm the bottom slightly and make it easier to remove the cheesecake from the pan. Blot any moisture that has accumulated on the surface of the cake with a paper towel, then sprinkle the surface of the cake with the granulated sugar. Take a deep breath! Invert a flat plate over the cheesecake and, in one fluid motion, turn the cheesecake out onto the plate. Carefully peel the parchment from the bottom of the cake, then set the baked crust on top of the cake. Invert a serving plate over the cake and (deep breath again!), in one fluid motion, invert the cake onto the serving platter so the crust is now on the bottom. With a sharp paring knife, trim any excess crust.

8. Cut the cake into wedges and serve.

KÓKUSZ TORTA
(Coconut-Marmalade Torte with Chocolate Glaze)

*Makes 1 rectangular cake;
serves 8 to 10*

FOR THE CAKE

2½ cups plus 2 tablespoons (300 grams) fine unsweetened dried coconut (sometimes called macaroon coconut)

2½ teaspoons tapioca flour (see page 21)

¼ teaspoon kosher salt

4 large eggs, plus 1 egg white

1 cup (198 grams) sugar

FOR ASSEMBLY

½ cup (149 grams) sour orange or kumquat marmalade, homemade (page 84 or 88) or store-bought

1 recipe Chocolate Glaze (recipe follows)

A handful of perfect pieces of large-flake unsweetened coconut (8 to 10 pieces), lightly toasted

Whipped Cream (page 330) for serving

Although coconut does not readily come to mind when you think of central European cakes, a mere cursory search results in numerous versions of coconut torten. I'm not a traditionalist per se, but I still like the cakes and tortes I serve in my cafe to represent what you might see in a *Konditorei* or *Kaffeehaus*.

In this cake, thin layers of pureed orange marmalade enhance the four layers of coconut "génoise," and the whole thing gets coated in chocolate glaze, bringing all the cake's elements into balance. I've tried using many different coconut flours for the cake, but I've found that whizzing regular unsweetened fine dried coconut in the food processor to make it a bit finer yields the best results.

1. **MAKE THE CAKE:** Preheat the oven to 350°F (175°C). Lightly grease two quarter sheet pans and line the pans with parchment.

2. Put the coconut in a food processor and pulse until the coconut is finely but not completely ground. You're not trying to make powdery coconut flour—imagine a tiny knife cutting each piece of coconut into halves or thirds. Transfer to a bowl and stir in the tapioca flour and salt.

3. Combine the eggs, egg white, and sugar in the bowl of your stand mixer (or in a large heatproof bowl) and set over a saucepan of simmering water. Cook, stirring, until the sugar has dissolved and the mixture is as hot as a hot bath (it should not be so hot that you cannot comfortably hold your finger in the eggs for a few seconds). Remove from the heat, transfer to the mixer stand, and fit it with the whisk attachment (or use a handheld mixer in the large bowl), and beat on high speed until the eggs are tripled in volume, pale in color, and cool, about 6 minutes. Remove the bowl from the mixer stand. If using, sprinkle one-third of the coconut mixture over the beaten eggs and fold in, then fold in the remaining coconut in 2 additions.

4. Transfer the batter to the prepared pans, dividing it evenly and using a small offset spatula to help spread it into the corners of each pan. It is important to work quickly here, because the batter will tighten up and get more difficult to spread as you go. (Don't be alarmed when this happens,

because it happens to me every time.) Give each pan a couple of firm raps on a counter lined with a towel. The towel is merely there to keep the noise down; the rapping is what evens out the batter.

5. Bake, rotating the pans once, until the cakes are golden brown and spring back slightly when touched, 15 to 20 minutes. Let cool completely in the pans on a wire rack.

6. Run an offset spatula around the edges of the cakes to loosen them from the pans. Place two sheets of parchment on the counter and invert each cake onto a sheet of parchment. Peel the parchment off the bottom of each cake, then cut each cake layer lengthwise in half. (This cake gets built with the bottom sides up, making a smoother surface for the finishing glaze).

7. **TO ASSEMBLE THE CAKE:** Pull out a few orange or kumquat pieces from the marmalade and reserve for garnish. Turn the remaining marmalade out onto a cutting board and finely chop. Heat the chocolate glaze over a pan of simmering water until spreadable.

8. Arrange one layer of coconut cake bottom side up on a wire rack set over a sheet pan. Spread with one-third of the marmalade, then top with a second cake layer, also bottom side up. Spread with half of the remaining marmalade, then top with another layer of cake. Spread the remaining marmalade on this cake layer, then top with the final layer of cake, bottom side up. Pour some of the chocolate glaze over the cake and, using an offset spatula, spread the glaze in a thin layer over the top and sides of the cake; it's okay if some of the cake is still visible beneath the glaze; this is just the crumb coat. Refrigerate the cake (still on its wire rack set over the pan) for 30 minutes.

9. Rewarm the remaining chocolate glaze until it has a pourable consistency. Remove the cake from the refrigerator and pour the glaze over it, letting the excess drip down the sides. Use an offset spatula to spread the glaze on the top into an even layer, then use the spatula to tidy up the appearance of the glaze on the sides of the cake. Sprinkle the top with the toasted coconut and dot with the reserved orange or kumquat pieces you stole from the marmalade (or you can wait until you slice the

cake and garnish each slice with a piece of the marmalade and a flake of coconut).

10. Transfer the cake to a serving platter and refrigerate until the glaze is set, about 30 minutes. Scoop up any glaze that has pooled in the pan beneath the cake and transfer to an airtight container; it can be reused and will keep, refrigerated, for many months. (*The cake can be refrigerated for up to a week.*)

11. When ready to serve the cake, bring to room temperature, then cut crosswise into 1-inch (2.5-centimeter) slices with a sharp knife. Serve with whipped cream.

Chocolate Glaze

*Makes a scant 2½ cups
(627 grams)*

10 ounces (285 grams)
72% cacao chocolate, such as
Valrhona Araguani, chopped

2 ounces (58 grams) 80% cacao
chocolate, such as Valrhona
Coeur de Guanaja, chopped

½ pound (224 grams) unsalted
butter

3 tablespoons (45 milliliters)
honey

Pinch of salt

1. Combine the chocolate, butter, honey, and salt in a large heatproof bowl. Set the bowl over a saucepan of simmering water, making sure the bottom of the bowl does not touch the water. Heat, stirring, until the chocolate and butter are about 80 percent melted, then remove from the heat and whisk until completely melted and smooth.

2. If using right away, set the bowl of glaze in a warm place to keep it fluid; I hold mine on top of the oven with a towel under it. Otherwise, let cool, then transfer to a lidded container and refrigerate until ready to use. The glaze will keep, refrigerated, for months; rewarm gently until fluid before using.

SACHER TORTE

*Makes one 9-inch
(23-centimeter) cake;
serves 8 to 10*

FOR THE CAKE

2½ cups (225 grams) almond meal (see page 17)

¼ cup plus ¼ teaspoon (30 grams) Dutch-process cocoa powder, such as Valrhona

¼ cup (35 grams) tapioca flour (see page 21)

8 large eggs

1½ cups plus 2 tablespoons (324 grams) sugar

¾ teaspoon kosher salt

6.4 ounces (183 grams) 72% cacao chocolate, such as Valrhona Araguani, chopped and melted over a bain-marie in a large folding bowl (see page 23) and kept warm enough to stay melted

1 recipe Chocolate Glaze (page 111), warmed until pourable

1 cup (237 milliliters) apricot jam, homemade (page 78) or store-bought, finely chopped or blitzed in a food processor (see Note)

Whipped Cream (page 330) for serving (optional)

I've heard many differing accounts of the origins of this cake, which is probably the most well known among all the cakes of central Europe. But I'll tell you the one I like best: In 1832, sixteen-year-old Franz Sacher, charged with the task of creating a special dessert for the distinguished guests of his employer, Prince Klemens von Metternich, developed the first iteration of this famous cake. Although the cake was purported to have delighted the guests, it wasn't until decades later that Franz's son, Eduard, perfected his father's recipe while completing his own pastry training at Demel bakery in Vienna. The cake was first served at Demel, and then later at the Hotel Sacher, established by Eduard Sacher in Vienna in 1876.

On my first trip to the Hotel Sacher, I was accompanied by the brilliant, fascinating Aimee Pavey, a fixture at the Castro Theater during San Francisco's Silent Film and Film Noir Festivals. To have Aimee as my real-life traveling companion on a trip centered around dressing up and eating cake in beautiful, grand rooms was a dream. She is not a chef or even a "foodie," but her innate curiosity about all things made her a most ideal dining companion, not to mention that she's blessed with a metabolism that makes it possible to have several meals of cake every day.

At the Hotel Sacher, we ordered, of course, two slices of the eponymous torte. Our immaculate slices arrived, and in perfect synchronicity, we picked up our forks and took our first bite. We looked at each other in confusion. We looked at the cake. We each took another bite. Aimee said, "It's dry?" I said, "I think it's supposed to be?"

The version here is more like what I dreamed a Sacher torte to be: a little more moist and a bit more chocolatey, but with the signature apricot filling in the center. A beautiful chocolate glaze finishes the cake.

I use the technique of heating the eggs and sugar together before whipping to yield maximum volume, then a slightly strange technique of folding the eggs into the melted chocolate, alternating with the dry ingredients. You may feel like you're doing it wrong, but the first addition of eggs is to loosen the chocolate, while the rest is to incorporate the dry ingredients.

This cake is very dark, and the top forms a strange, bumpy crust during baking, so traditional methods for testing doneness are no good here. A trick I learned from a great baker, Julia Stockton, is to listen to the cake: The bubbles popping in the batter make a sound, and the cake will be silent when it is done. But please be careful not to burn your face as you hold the cake close to your ear, listening for doneness.

1. **MAKE THE CAKE:** Preheat the oven to 325°F (165°C). Grease the bottom of two 9-inch (23-centimeter) round cake pans and line with parchment.

2. With a tamis or sifter, sift the almond meal, cocoa powder, and tapioca flour into a medium bowl.

3. Combine the eggs, sugar, and salt in the bowl of a stand mixer (or in a large heatproof bowl). Set the bowl over a saucepan of simmering water, making sure the bottom of the bowl does not touch the water, and whisk until the mixture is hot (like a hot bath, not a vat of molten lava) to the touch.

4. Attach the bowl to the mixer stand, fitted with the whisk attachment (or use the large bowl and a handheld mixer), and whip on high speed until the eggs are pale and tripled in volume, about 6 minutes. Fold the egg mixture into the chocolate in 3 additions, alternating with the dry ingredients, folding gently but quickly so the mixture stays warm. Divide the batter evenly between the prepared pans.

5. Bake the cake for 45 minutes. Remove one layer from the oven and listen; you may hear the sound of bubbles popping. If so, return the pan to the oven and continue baking, removing and listening every 5 minutes, until the cake is quiet. This can take as long as an hour, so don't fret if it does! Let the layers cool in their pans on a wire rack.

6. Once the layers are cool, run a small offset spatula, with the front of it facing outward, around the edges of each one, pressing the spatula against the pan so you don't cut into the cake, then turn out onto the cooling rack and flip top side up. With a large serrated knife, cut off the crispy top of each cake layer; reserve the trimmings.

7. Crumble the cake trimmings into fine crumbs. In a small bowl, combine a few handfuls of the crumbs with enough of the chocolate glaze to make a thick paste.

(continued)

8. **TO ASSEMBLE THE CAKE:** Place one cake layer (top side up) on a wire rack and top with the apricot jam, spreading it in an even layer all the way to the edges. Top with the second cake layer, bottom side up. Use the crumb paste to spackle the gap between the two layers, smoothing it out with an offset spatula. Don't fret if you need to make a smidgen more paste; you may need a little or a lot, depending on how wide the gap is, so don't start snacking on your crumbs until the sides of the cake are smooth.

9. Set the cake, still on its wire rack, over a sheet pan and pour the warm glaze evenly over it, letting the excess drip down the sides of the cake and onto the sheet pan.

10. When the cake is covered with the glaze, use a large spatula (or two!) to transfer it to a serving platter and refrigerate until the glaze is set, about 30 minutes. With a rubber spatula, scrape up the glaze that pooled on the baking sheet and transfer to a lidded container. It will keep, refrigerated, for many months. (*The cake can be refrigerated for up to a week.*)

11. To serve, cut the cake into wedges and garnish each slice with a generous dollop of whipped cream, if desired.

NOTE: To provide a sneak peek at the filling within, I sometimes garnish each slice of cake with a piece of apricot that I've fished out of my jar of homemade jam. You can do the same, or just serve the slices unadorned.

WALNUT-APRICOT TORTE

*Makes 1 rectangular cake;
serves 8 to 10*

FOR THE CAKE

1¼ cups (100 grams) walnuts, toasted and cooled (toast the walnut halves for garnish at the same time)

¼ teaspoon kosher salt

¼ cup plus 2 tablespoons (45 grams) all-purpose flour

⅓ cup (29 grams) almond meal (see page 17)

¼ cup plus 3 tablespoons (71 grams) confectioners' sugar

10 tablespoons (143 grams) unsalted butter, plus more for greasing the pan

4 large egg whites, at room temperature

⅛ teaspoon cream of tartar

¼ cup (49 grams) sugar

FOR THE SHORTBREAD CRUST

2½ tablespoons (35 grams) unsalted butter, melted and cooled

1½ tablespoons granulated sugar

¼ teaspoon kosher salt

2½ tablespoons (35 grams) unsalted butter, very soft

½ cup plus 2 tablespoons (75 grams) all-purpose flour, sifted

(continued)

This recipe was inspired by a cake made by the mother of my former assistant, Hili Rezvan. Hili's mama's cake was unlike anything I had ever tasted before. The flavors weren't particularly unusual, but somehow the combination of layers really struck a chord with me. The texture of the cake was crumbly but also cakey. Not dry, and not moist either. Not like a cookie, and not like a pastry crust. It wasn't long, and it wasn't short, it was just a squat little rectangle. There were four thin layers of cake with an apricot jam sandwiched between them, all cloaked with a dark chocolate glaze.

The cake itself has become somewhat mythological to me, so my memory of it is hazy, but not the memory of its impact. It's not an overstatement to say that this cake started me on my path to creating the 20th Century Cafe. If Hili hadn't shared her mother's cake with me, I'd never have traveled to eastern Europe, I'd never have learned about the pastries and cakes of that region, and I'd never have been inspired to make my own version of those grand cafes. It truly is the wellspring from which everything else came.

Hili's mother learned to bake from her mother, who was raised in Hungary. I learned that zerbo, which is what Hili's mom, who is from Israel, called the cake, is the same as Gerbeaud, a cake named after the famous pastry shop in Budapest. Or maybe vice versa. And even though this cake isn't too much like zerbo or Gerbeaud, it was inspired by that cake from Hili, and it is the cake that, more than any other, inspires my customers to exclaim, "My grandmother made this cake!"

My version of the torte has a shortbread crust (which can be made ahead and chilled overnight or frozen for a month, then baked the day of assembly) and two layers of walnut–brown butter cake sandwiched with apricot jam, and it is finished with dark chocolate glaze.

1. **MAKE THE CAKE:** Preheat the oven to 375°F (190°C). Butter a quarter sheet pan and line with parchment.

2. Spread the toasted walnuts on another quarter sheet pan and freeze for 10 minutes. Transfer the nuts to the bowl of a food processor, add the salt, and process until coarsely chopped. Add the flour and almond meal and process until the nuts are finely ground, stopping the processor periodically and scraping down the sides to avoid making walnut butter. Add the

About ½ cup (118 milliliters) Chocolate Glaze (page 111), warmed until pourable

1¼ cups (296 milliliters) apricot jam, homemade (page 78) or store-bought

A few walnut halves, toasted (from above) and cooled

Flaky sea salt, such as Maldon, for sprinkling

Whipped Cream (page 330) for serving (optional)

confectioners' sugar and continue processing until the mixture is a fine, dry powder.

3. To make the brown butter, put the butter in a small saucepan. (You begin with a little more butter than you will need for the recipe; there will be some loss due to evaporation, and any that's left over can be sopped up with bread for a snack.) Set out a bowl of ice, large enough to put the bottom of your small saucepan in. Heat the butter over medium heat until it melts and separates. Then begin whisking. It will get foamy, and eventually creamy and bubbly, and then it will begin to separate again. Keep whisking. It will start to take on some color and foam up, and it will be difficult to see what is happening with the color, so use your nose here. As soon as the butter smells like hazelnuts, pull it off the heat, whisking all the while, and set the saucepan in the bowl of ice to stop the cooking. Keep whisking until the heat has dissipated. Measure out 9 tablespoons (128 grams) of the browned butter; it should be still liquid but not hot when you add it to the cake batter.

4. In the bowl of a stand mixer fitted with the whisk attachment (or in a large bowl, using a handheld mixer), beat the egg whites on low speed until foamy. Add the cream of tartar and gradually increase the mixer speed. When the whites begin to look somewhat opaque, gradually add the granulated sugar and continue whipping until the egg whites hold medium-firm peaks. Transfer the beaten whites to a large bowl and fold in the dry ingredients in 4 additions, not fully incorporating each addition before adding the next. Add one-third of the warm (but not hot) brown butter at the end of the third addition of dry ingredients, another third during the fourth addition of dry ingredients, and the remaining third after all the dry ingredients have been added, folding gently but thoroughly until the batter is homogeneous.

5. Pour the batter into the prepared pan and use a small offset spatula to spread it evenly in the pan, working it as little as possible. Tap the pan on the counter to pop any large air bubbles.

6. Bake for 16 minutes, then rotate the pan and bake for another 6 to 8 minutes, until the cake is golden, starts to pulls away from the edges of the

DATE-PISTACHIO TORTE

*Makes 1 rectangular cake;
serves 10*

FOR THE SHORTBREAD

⅓ cup (66 grams) sugar

½ teaspoon ground cardamom

¾ teaspoon kosher salt

8 tablespoons (113 grams) unsalted butter, melted and cooled

8 tablespoons (113 grams) unsalted butter, very soft

2 cups (240 grams) all-purpose flour

½ teaspoon baking powder

FOR THE FILLING

1¼ pounds (567 grams) dates, such as Barhi or Medjool (see page 18), pitted

1 tablespoon brewed espresso or coffee

1 tablespoon tangerine or orange juice

FOR THE HONEY BUTTERCREAM

3 large egg yolks

⅓ cup plus 1 tablespoon (90 milliliters) honey

Pinch of kosher salt

12 tablespoons (169 grams) unsalted butter, very soft

¾ teaspoon rose water (see page 21)

(continued)

Although this torte has none of the same elements that make up the famous Gerbeaud cake (see Walnut-Apricot Torte, page 117), to me it somehow feels like a San Francisco version of that storied treat. It is a sophisticated dessert with a gentle sweetness. It's made of four layers of cardamom-scented pastry sandwiched with a coffee-date jam, and the whole thing is topped with honey buttercream. The pastry recipe may look familiar; I just lightened the shortbread that forms the bottom layer of the Plum Kuchen (page 55) and the Walnut-Apricot Torte with a little baking powder and added some ground cardamom. The baked pastry is very delicate, so be careful when spreading it with the date jam, and use a large offset spatula, or the bottom of a removable-bottomed tart pan, to lift and stack the layers.

1. **MAKE THE SHORTBREAD:** In a wide glass or stainless steel bowl, whisk together the sugar, cardamom, and salt. Furiously whisk in the melted butter; the mixture will emulsify, resembling mayonnaise. Whisk in the soft butter. Combine the flour and baking powder and add to the butter mixture all at once. Using your hand like a claw, rake through the mixture until the flour is completely incorporated and the dough is homogeneous. This should be fun, and not much work.

2. Transfer the dough to a sheet of parchment, top with a second sheet of parchment, and roll into a 15¾-by-10¼-inch (40-by-26-centimeter) rectangle. Place the dough, still on the parchment, on a sheet pan and refrigerate for 30 minutes.

3. Preheat the oven to 300°F (150°C).

4. Cut the dough (still on the parchment) crosswise into 4 equal rectangles. Bake for 15 minutes, then reduce the oven temperature to 250°F (120°C). Use the palm of your hand to gently pat down any bubbles that may have begun to form. Then continue baking until the shortbread is dark golden brown, 10 to 15 minutes longer. Let cool fully on the pan on a wire rack.

5. **MEANWHILE, MAKE THE FILLING:** If using a variety of dates other than Barhi (which are very soft and do not require soaking), put the dates in a glass jar or narrow bowl, add just enough very hot water to barely cover, and soak for 15 minutes, or until the dates are very soft. Drain, reserving the soaking liquid, and transfer to the bowl of a food processor. Add the

DOBOS TORTA

*Makes one 9-inch
(23-centimeter) cake; serves
16 to 18*

FOR THE CAKE

18 tablespoons (254 grams) unsalted butter, at room temperature

6 tablespoons (48 grams) confectioners' sugar

½ teaspoon baking powder

¼ teaspoon kosher salt

Grated zest of 1 Meyer lemon

8 large eggs, separated

1 cup plus 6 tablespoons (170 grams) cake or pastry flour

½ teaspoon cream of tartar

¾ cup plus 2 tablespoons (168 grams) granulated sugar

FOR ASSEMBLY

1 recipe Chocolate Buttercream (recipe follows), at room temperature

1 cup (198 grams) granulated sugar

Flaky sea salt, such as Maldon, for sprinkling

A chunk of unsalted butter for coating the knife when scoring the caramel

The Dobos torta is among the most famous, most impressive cakes from the Austro-Hungarian Empire. It's still a staple of many cafes, particularly in Budapest. There's a lot of controversy about the number of layers in a traditional Dobos torta. Some people say five, some say seven, some say even more, but I like the way seven looks, so that's what I recommend.

The cake is tender but has a slightly sandy, chewy texture that sets it apart from a traditional sponge cake. The buttercream is intensely chocolatey, with a touch of caramel that foreshadows the extravagant traditional caramel top. The addition of salt, though not traditional, was requested by the cake, and I always listen to my food (if not my husband). The decorative top layer can be challenging and a little bit stressful because the window of opportunity to be able to cut the caramel-covered pieces is very brief. But it's worth the effort, sweat, and yelling: The caramel "fan" crowning the cake is one of the things that makes a Dobos torta a Dobos torta.

Be sure to make plenty of space on your counters to put all the layers while they wait their turns in the oven; there are eight of them (seven layers for the torte and an eighth that gets coated in caramel for a decorative topper), and the batter needs to be divvied up and spread as soon as the egg whites are folded in. You might have a tiny kitchen, but use your imagination (and don't forget to bake the one you put on top of the refrigerator!). You can make and frost the cake a day or two before you plan to serve it, but don't add the caramel-coated garnish until shortly before you serve it; it would get tacky in the refrigerator.

1. Preheat the oven to 350°F (175°C). With a dark marker, trace eight 9-inch (23-centimeter) circles onto eight 11-by-17-inch (28-by-44-centimeter) sheets of parchment, then flip the sheets over.

2. In the bowl of a stand mixer fitted with the paddle attachment (or in a large bowl, using a handheld mixer), cream the butter, confectioners' sugar, baking powder, and salt on medium-high speed until light and fluffy, about 4 minutes. Add the lemon zest, then reduce the speed to medium and add the egg yolks one at a time, mixing well after each addition. Transfer the mixture to a large bowl and fold in the cake flour in 3 additions. Wash and dry the mixer bowl if using a stand mixer.

3. In the bowl of the stand mixer, fitted with the whisk attachment (or in another large bowl, using the handheld mixer, with clean beaters), whip

the egg whites on low speed until foamy. Add the cream of tartar, then gradually increase the mixer speed and slowly add the granulated sugar. Whip until the whites hold stiff peaks. Whisk one-third of the beaten egg whites into the batter to loosen it, then gently fold in the remaining egg whites in 2 additions.

4. Scoop the batter onto the sheets of parchment (an ice cream scoop is a handy tool), dividing it evenly and placing it in the center of the circles you drew on the paper. (Look, I'm supposed to be a fancy pastry chef, and I just eyeball it, so just do your best to be accurate. It's gonna be amazing no matter what!) With a small offset spatula, spread the batter in a thin, even layer, filling the circles.

5. Place 2 of the sheets of parchment on sheet pans and bake until the layers are golden brown and spring back when touched, 10 to 12 minutes, rotating the pans halfway through baking. Slide the layers off the pans to cool on a flat surface. Repeat with the remaining layers, noting that the baking time may decrease with subsequent layers, since the pans are already warm. Be sure to set one of your layers away from where you will be assembling the cake—I have in fact accidentally frosted my intended caramel layer and then had to make a whole new batch of cake just to get another top.

6. **TO ASSEMBLE THE CAKE:** Run a large offset spatula under each cake layer to free it from the parchment. Arrange one cake layer on a serving plate and top with about a heaping ½ cup (115 to 125 grams) of the buttercream. Using a small offset spatula, spread it into a thin, even layer. Repeat with 6 more layers. Transfer a few tablespoons of the buttercream to a piping bag fitted with a small star tip and set aside, then frost the top and sides of the cake with the remaining buttercream. Transfer the cake to the refrigerator and refrigerate for at least 30 minutes to set the buttercream. (*The cake can be refrigerated for up to 3 days. Let come to room temperature before making the caramel triangles and garnishing the cake.*)

7. When the buttercream is set, remove the cake from the fridge and, with a knife, make very light marks on top of the cake to divide it into 16 or 18 wedges. Pipe a small rosette of the reserved buttercream onto the middle of each wedge.

(continued)

FLÓDNI

*Makes one 9-inch
(23-centimeter) cake;
serves 12 to 16*

FOR THE PASTRY

2¼ cups (270 grams) all-purpose flour

2 cups (240 grams) bread flour

½ cup (99 grams) sugar

1½ teaspoons kosher salt

1¼ pounds (567 grams) cold unsalted butter, cut into pats ¼ inch (0.5 centimeter) thick

1 large egg yolk

FOR ASSEMBLY

1 recipe Poppy Seed Filling (recipe follows), at room temperature

1 recipe Walnut Filling (recipe follows), at room temperature

1 recipe Plum Lekvar (page //), at room temperature

1 recipe Apple Butter (see page 141), cooked to reduce to 2 cups, at room temperature

1 large egg, beaten, for egg wash

Whipped Cream (page 330) for serving

Unlike many of the other cakes in this chapter, flódni isn't seen much outside of Budapest, or at least it won't be called flódni. I tried a similar cake in Vienna, at Café Frauenhuber. When I asked the waiter if it was flódni, he insisted, "No, it is Haustorte." "But does it have another name?" I pressed, trying to determine if it was, in fact, the same cake. "Yes. Haustorte."

A multilayered affair, typically prepared for special celebrations, flódni is not for the weak. Not only is the cake physically heavy (it takes over an hour to bake), it also requires that you make four distinct fillings, as well as a pastry dough. But I assure you that your labors will be worthwhile; the finished cake is much greater than the sum of its parts. With no frosting to entice you, flódni can look, well, a bit homely. But when you slice into it, revealing the four layers, your guests will go wild. Make the fillings in advance (they'll keep for several days in the refrigerator); it's too much work to make this cake all in one day.

1. **MAKE THE PASTRY LAYERS:** Preheat the oven to 325°F (165°C).

2. In the bowl of a stand mixer fitted with the paddle attachment (or in a large bowl, using a handheld mixer), combine the flours, sugar, and salt and mix on low speed. With the mixer on low, drop in the pats of butter and continue mixing until the butter is in quarter-size pieces. Add the egg yolk and mix just until a dough forms.

3. Transfer the dough to a lightly floured work surface and, with a bench scraper or a knife, divide it into five 6½-ounce (184-gram) pieces and one 9-ounce (255-gram) piece.

4. On a lightly floured surface, with a lightly floured rolling pin, working with one piece of dough at a time, roll the 5 smaller pieces of dough into 8½-inch (22-centimeter) rounds, making 2 just a little larger than the other 3 (these larger rounds will be your top and bottom). Transfer to sheets of parchment and chill. Divide the remaining piece of dough in half and roll each half into a rectangle that is 2½ by 14½ inches (6.5 by 37 centimeters). Transfer to a sheet of parchment and chill.

5. Transfer 3 of the rounds, still on the parchment, to sheet pans (2 rounds side by side on one sheet of parchment on one pan, and the third one on a separate pan) and bake until golden, about 20 minutes. Remove from

PUDDINGS, CUSTARDS, AND ICE CREAMS

Back row, from left to right: Kávé Becsipett Sherry Trifle (page 163); Strawberry Ice Cream (see page 193);
Hibiscus Iced Tea, Peach, and Peach Leaf Ice Cream Float (page 183); Chicory Ice Cream (page 184);
Coconut Bavarian with Tangerine Granita and Basil Seeds (page 167); Front row, from left to right: Poppy
Seed Ice Cream (page 188), Black Walnut Ice Cream (page 189), Lemon Verbena Sherbet (page 179),
Cardamom Ice Cream (page 180), Buttermilk Panna Cotta (page 169), Butterscotch Pudding (page 174),
Coconut Rice Pudding Baked in a Fig Leaf (page 173)

KÁVÉ BECSÍPETT SHERRY TRIFLE

Serves 10 to 12

FOR THE CAKE

2 tablespoons (28 grams) unsalted butter, plus more for greasing the pan

4 large eggs, at room temperature

½ cup (99 grams) sugar

⅛ teaspoon kosher salt

1 cup (120 grams) cake or pastry flour, sifted

FOR THE SHERRY SYRUP

1 cup (237 milliliters) hot freshly brewed coffee

¾ cup (165 grams) Demerara sugar (see page 21)

1½ cups (355 milliliters) Oloroso sherry

FOR THE MEYER LEMON MOUSSE

4 Meyer lemons

2 large eggs

4 large egg yolks

½ cup (99 grams) granulated sugar

10 tablespoons (143 grams) cold unsalted butter, cut into cubes

2 cups (473 milliliters) heavy cream

(continued)

This festive dessert was inspired by a cocktail called the kávé becsípett, which is Hungarian for "tipsy coffee." The trifle is made with a simple, perfect génoise—a recipe I learned from the late and very best baker Flo Braker—infused with a copious amount of sherry and layered with a Meyer lemon cream. For the sherry syrup, I like to use a fruity-nosed single-origin coffee and Oloroso sherry, which is known for its rich, nutty flavor. The trifle can be made up to three days ahead.

1. **MAKE THE CAKE:** Adjust a rack to the lower third of the oven and preheat the oven to 350°F (175°C). Grease and flour an 8-inch (20-centimeter) round cake pan and line with parchment.

2. Melt the butter in a medium saucepan over low heat. Pour into a medium bowl; set nearby. Rinse the saucepan.

3. Put the eggs, sugar, and salt in the bowl of a stand mixer (or a large heat-proof bowl). Set the bowl over the saucepan filled with just-simmering water, making sure the bottom of the bowl doesn't touch the water, and lightly whisk until the mixture is hot, like bathwater. Remove from the heat. Using the whisk attachment (or a handheld mixer), whip the eggs until tripled in volume, 4 to 5 minutes. Remove the bowl from the mixer stand (if using a stand mixer) and fold in the flour in 3 additions, mixing until just incorporated.

4. Pour about one-third of the batter into the melted butter and fold just until combined, then fold into the remaining batter. Pour the batter into the prepared pan and spread evenly.

5. Bake the cake until the top springs back slightly when lightly touched, about 25 minutes. Cool for 10 minutes, then run a knife around the edges of the cake and invert it onto a wire rack. Cool completely

6. **MAKE THE SHERRY SYRUP:** In a small bowl, whisk together the coffee and Demerara sugar until the sugar is dissolved, then add the sherry. Refrigerate until thoroughly chilled. (*The syrup can be refrigerated, covered, for up to a week.*)

(continued)

COCONUT BAVARIAN WITH TANGERINE GRANITA AND BASIL SEEDS

Serves 6 to 8

FOR THE BAVARIAN

2 cups (473 milliliters) heavy cream

½ cup (57 grams) fine unsweetened dried coconut (sometimes called macaroon coconut), toasted

2¼ sheets bronze-strength gelatin (see page 19)

One 13.5- to 14-ounce (398- to 414-milliliter) can full-fat coconut milk

3 tablespoons (36 grams) sugar

¼ teaspoon kosher salt

2 to 3 teaspoons basil seeds (see headnote)

Tangerine Granita (page 73) for serving

A Bavarian is a chilled custard dessert made by setting liquid (usually milk, but in this case, coconut milk) with gelatin or eggs, then folding in whipped cream. It is light, refreshing, pretty, and super fun to eat. You can find basil seeds in Asian markets. When soaked in water, they plump up like little tiny eyeballs, but, you know, in an appealing sort of way, adding an interesting texture to this creamy Bavarian. Everything can be prepped ahead, including the coconut cream, which, in fact, needs to steep overnight, and the dessert looks very fancy with little effort.

If you don't want to make the Tangerine Granita, you can serve the Bavarian with a scoop of good-quality sorbet or sherbet on top; even a couple of spoonfuls of lightly sweetened tangerine juice poured over the soaked basil seeds just before serving would be lovely.

1. **MAKE THE BAVARIAN:** In a small saucepan, warm the cream over medium heat until bubbles appear at the edges of the pan. Stir in the toasted coconut, remove from the heat, and let cool, then transfer to a lidded container and refrigerate overnight.

2. The next day, put the gelatin sheets in a bowl and add cold water to cover.

3. In a medium saucepan, combine the coconut milk, sugar, and salt. Cook over medium heat, stirring, until the sugar has dissolved and the mixture is hot to the touch. Remove from the heat and pour into a large bowl. Remove the gelatin sheets from the bowl of water and squeeze gently to extract excess water. Add to the bowl with the warm coconut milk and whisk to melt and incorporate. Let cool to room temperature, then refrigerate until cold.

4. Remove the steeped coconut cream from the refrigerator and strain through a fine-mesh strainer, pressing hard on the solids. Transfer the cream to the bowl of a stand mixer fitted with the whisk attachment (or use a large bowl and a handheld mixer) and beat until the cream holds soft peaks. Stir one-third of the cream into the chilled coconut milk base, then fold in the remaining whipped coconut cream in 2 additions. (If the coconut Jell-O is firm, whisk until smooth before folding in the cream.)

(continued)

COCONUT RICE PUDDING BAKED IN A FIG LEAF

Serves 8

FOR THE PUDDING

Two 13.5- to 14-ounce (398- to 414-milliliter) cans full-fat coconut milk

1 cup (227 grams) water

5 tablespoons (62 grams) sugar

¼ teaspoon kosher salt

½ cup (99 grams) short-grain rice

8 fresh fig leaves (optional; see headnote)

2 peaches, halved, pitted, and thinly sliced into wedges

1 teaspoon sugar

½ cup (60 grams) raspberries

Versions of rice pudding exist across almost all food cultures, though it has particularly strong ties to Sephardic Jewish cuisine. This rendition, made without eggs or dairy, is a perfect Passover dessert.

Coconut milk is used here in place of the traditional whole milk, and the fig leaves impart a subtle flavor, lending depth to the richness of the coconut milk. Freshly sliced peaches add juiciness, raspberries give a tart pop, and both echo the floral qualities of the pudding. If you can't find fresh fig leaves, the pudding is still delicious simply spooned warm from the pot into serving bowls with the peaches and berries.

1. **MAKE THE PUDDING:** In a medium saucepan, combine the coconut milk, water, sugar, and salt and bring to a simmer over medium heat. Stir in the rice and gently simmer, stirring occasionally, for 30 minutes. Cover the pan and cook for 10 minutes more, until the liquid is visibly thickened and the rice is swollen and tender. Remove from the heat and let cool slightly.

2. Preheat the oven to 350°F (175°C). Line eight 8-ounce (237-milliliter) ramekins with the fig leaves, if you have them.

3. Divide the pudding among the ramekins, then fold the edges of the leaves, if you're using them, around each portion of pudding, enclosing it completely. (*The puddings can be prepared ahead to this point and refrigerated for up to 1 day.*)

4. Set the ramekins on a sheet pan, transfer to the oven, and bake for 15 minutes, until the pudding is hot.

5. **WHILE THE PUDDING BAKES, PREPARE THE PEACHES:** In a medium bowl, combine the peaches with the sugar. Let stand for 5 minutes, or until juicy.

6. To unmold, one at a time, hold each ramekin with a dry towel and invert the fig-leaf-wrapped (or not) parcel onto a large spatula. Remove the ramekin, then flip the pudding onto a serving plate or into a bowl, so the opening faces up. Open the pudding parcels and top each with a few peach slices and a few raspberries. Serve immediately.

BUTTERSCOTCH PUDDING

Serves 8

5 tablespoons (70 grams) unsalted butter

¼ cup plus 2 teaspoons (56 grams) packed dark brown sugar

¼ cup (56 grams) packed light Muscovado sugar (see page 21)

1 cup plus 2 tablespoons (267 milliliters) heavy cream

1¾ sheets bronze-strength gelatin (see page 19)

1 cup plus 2 tablespoons (267 milliliters) whole milk

3 large egg yolks

2 teaspoons dark rum

½ teaspoon kosher salt

Vanilla Cream (page 330) for serving

Chopped Toffee (page 235) for serving (optional but strongly recommended)

The word "butterscotch" has such a wonderful ring to it, but I've always found butterscotch things very unappealing. Butterscotch chips, butterscotch pudding, butterscotch candy—how can something that sounds so delicious taste so bad? I was determined to make butterscotch pudding that *was* delicious. It was my husband, Franz, not an old cookbook, who cracked the code. He was reading a Wikipedia entry on the etymology of the word, and when he said, "Butter*scorch*," I knew I had my man. *I mean*, pudding.

1. In a medium saucepan, combine 2½ tablespoons of the butter, the brown sugar, and Muscovado sugar and cook over medium-high heat, stirring, until the mixture lets out a few puffs of smoke.

2. Remove the pan from the heat and whisk in the remaining 2½ tablespoons butter, which will stop the cooking. Whisk in the cream, then blend with an immersion blender until smooth (or whisk like hell until your arm falls off). Transfer to a large bowl and let cool. (*This step can be done a day ahead; transfer the mixture to a lidded container and store in the refrigerator.*)

3. Place the gelatin sheets in a bowl and add cold water to cover.

4. In a large saucepan, whisk together the milk and egg yolks and cook over medium heat, stirring, until the mixture registers 175°F (77°C) on an instant-read thermometer. Remove from the heat and stir in the rum and salt, then strain through a fine-mesh strainer into a clean bowl.

5. Remove the gelatin sheets from the bowl of water and squeeze gently to extract excess water. Add to the bowl with the warm custard and stir until melted and incorporated. Whisk in the cooled cream mixture.

6. Divide the pudding among eight small ramekins, glass jars, pudding dishes, or bowls and refrigerate until cold and set, at least 2 hours, or up to overnight. (*The pudding will keep for up to 4 days in the refrigerator, but you should wrap it tightly to prevent it from picking up off flavors.*)

7. Serve the pudding cold, topped with vanilla cream and chopped toffee, if desired.

LEMON VERBENA SHERBET

*Makes 1 quart
(950 milliliters)*

¾ cup (149 grams) sugar

½ cup (118 milliliters) water

2 tablespoons (30 milliliters) honey

About 2 handfuls loosely packed lemon verbena leaves (see page 19)

3 cups (710 milliliters) plain whole-milk yogurt

Pinch of kosher salt

Creamy, light, and super refreshing, this frozen treat is delicious with any summer fruit as a dessert, or as a palate-cleansing course in the middle of a spicy meal. The flavor is quite intense, and not for everyone, but it's one of my favorites. If you can't find lemon verbena leaves at your local store, look online, ask for them at your farmers' market, or grow your own plant.

Because there are no eggs to prevent this sherbet from icing up, it is best to serve it within a day of making it, to keep the creamy texture. If needed, you can always melt it gently and churn it again before serving.

1. In a medium saucepan, combine the sugar, water, and honey and bring to a boil, stirring to dissolve the sugar. Remove from the heat, transfer to a bowl, and chill.

2. Once the honey mixture is cold, pour into a blender and add the lemon verbena. Blend thoroughly, then strain through a fine-mesh strainer into a medium bowl. Whisk in the yogurt and add the salt.

3. Process the mixture in your ice cream maker according to the manufacturer's instructions, then transfer to a freezer container and freeze until firm. This sherbet is best eaten within a day of being made.

From left to right: Hibiscus Iced Tea, Peach, and Peach Leaf Ice Cream Float
(page 183); Chicory Ice Cream (page 184); Hibiscus Iced Tea with Peach
Leaf Ice Cream (page 182); Brown Butter–Toffee Shortbread (page 209)

From left to right: Poppy Seed Ice Cream
(page 188); Black Walnut Ice Cream (page 189)

with a wooden spoon until the mixture comes together in a ball. Continue to cook for 1 to 2 minutes more, until there is a film on the bottom of the saucepan. Remove from the heat and stir vigorously with the spoon to release some of the steam, then beat in the eggs one at a time.

7. Transfer the dough to a piping bag fitted with a ½-inch (1.5-centimeter) plain tip. Pipe a dozen 1½-inch (4-centimeter) mounds onto the baking sheets, leaving about 1 inch (2.5 centimeters) between them.

8. Bake until deep golden brown and puffed, 22 to 24 minutes. Remove from the oven and poke the side of each cream puff with a wooden skewer to release the steam. Transfer to a wire rack and let cool.

9. When you're ready to serve the ice cream puffs, remove the ice cream from the freezer to soften. Cut each puff crosswise in half and place a small scoop of ice cream on the bottom half of each one. Replace the tops of the puffs. Place 2 puffs on each of six serving plates. If desired, drizzle some chocolate sauce around the puffs, dollop with whipped cream, and sprinkle with chopped pistachio praline. Serve immediately.

Roasted Strawberries

Makes about 1 cup
(310 grams)

2 pounds (908 grams) strawberries, hulled, halved if large

⅔ to ¾ cup (132 to 150 grams) sugar

1. Preheat the oven to 300°F (150°C).

2. Arrange the strawberries in a single layer in a shallow glass or ceramic baking dish, sprinkle with the sugar (the amount of sugar you'll need depends on the sweetness of your berries—taste them to see!), and mix briefly. Roast, stirring every hour, until the strawberries shrink significantly and the juices they release have reduced to a syrup, about 3 hours. Let cool to room temperature.

3. Transfer the strawberries and their juices to an airtight container and store in the fridge for up to 4 days.

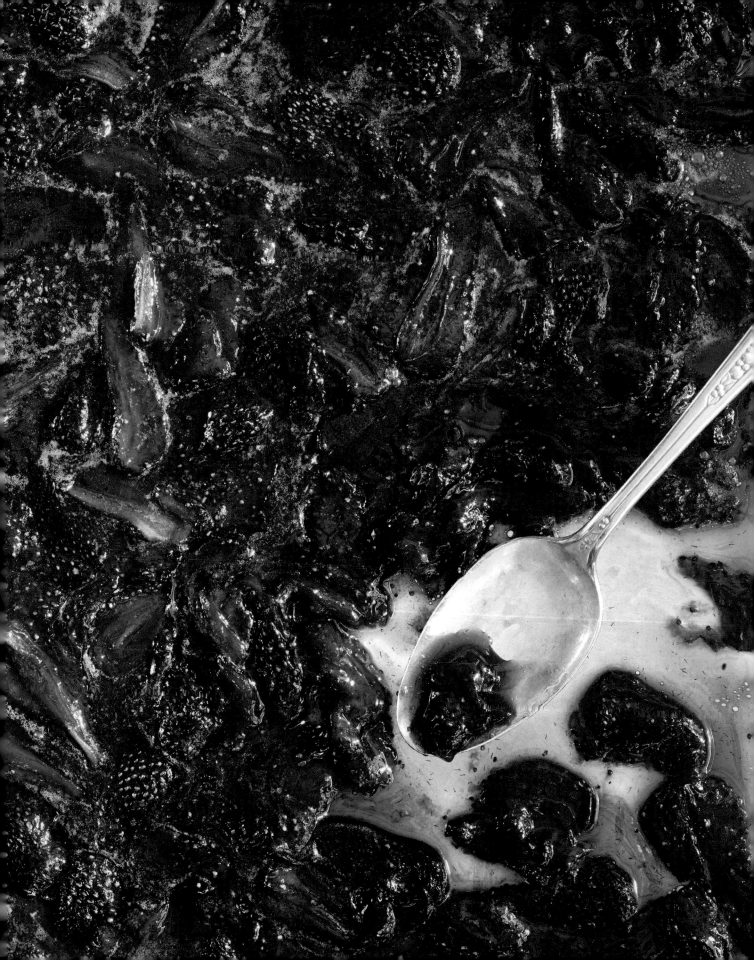

Hot chocolate (left; page 196) and Hot Butterscotch (right; page 197),
served with Vanilla Kipferl (page 215)

COOKIES
AND
CANDIES

Back row, from left to right: Cacao Nib Meringue Kisses (page 207), Linzer Augen (page 227), Black Walnut and Buckwheat Russian Tea Cakes (page 211), Plum Kiffels (page 221), Cacao Nib Sandwich Cookies (page 229); Front row, from left to right: Chocolate Truffles (page 230), Candied Grapefruit Peel (page 232), Toffee (page 235), Caraway Seed Shortbread (page 208), Poppy Seed Rugelach (page 219); Brown Butter–Toffee Shortbread (page 209), Vanilla Kipferl (page 215), Hamantaschen (see page 225), Bulgarian Shortbread (page 217)

CACAO NIB MERINGUE KISSES

Makes about 70 tiny kisses

2 large egg whites

1 cup (114 grams) confectioners' sugar

½ teaspoon kosher salt

¼ cup (30 grams) cacao nibs (see page 17)

When you find yourself with extra egg whites, this versatile recipe is a great way to use them up. Cacao nibs keep the sweetness of the meringue in check; you could also flavor these with ground espresso, or rose water, or many other things. You can make big, chewy kisses, but I like to make smaller ones that are light and crunchy and keep for weeks. Crush them and layer in a pretty glass with fresh berries and whipped cream. You can even spread the meringue thin and bake it to cut into squares or rectangles to make a base and top for ice cream sandwiches. Didn't I say versatile?

1. Preheat the oven to 325°F (165°C). Line two sheet pans with parchment or silicone baking mats.

2. Combine the egg whites, sugar, and salt in the bowl of a stand mixer (or in a medium heatproof bowl). Bring 1 inch (2.5 centimeters) of water to a simmer in a saucepan and set the bowl over the simmering water, making sure the bottom of the bowl is not touching the water. Heat, whisking, until the sugar is dissolved and the mixture is hot to the touch. Transfer the bowl to the mixer stand, fitted with the whisk attachment (or use a handheld mixer in the medium bowl), and beat on high speed until the mixture is very thick and holds stiff, glossy peaks. Fold in the cacao nibs.

3. Transfer the meringue to a piping bag fitted with a small plain tip and pipe on the prepared sheet pans, making small mounds about ¾ inch (2 centimeters) in diameter, spaced about 1 inch (2.5 centimeters) apart. (You can pipe whichever size you like, but be sure to adjust the baking time if you make them a different size.)

4. Place the sheet pans in the oven and prop the oven door slightly ajar with the handle of a wooden spoon. Bake until the cookies are puffed and cracking on the sides and feel dry on the outside but still squishy within, 12 to 15 minutes; they'll harden as they cool. If you want them to be crunchy all the way through, turn off the oven and let them dry out for 5 to 10 more minutes. If you can easily pull one from the paper or mat, they are done.

5. Transfer the meringues to a wire rack and let cool completely. The cookies will keep in an airtight container for up to a week.

CARAWAY SEED SHORTBREAD

Pictured on page 213

Makes about 2 dozen cookies

¾ teaspoon caraway seeds

½ pound (227 grams) unsalted butter, very soft

⅓ cup (66 grams) sugar, plus 1 tablespoon for dusting

¾ teaspoon kosher salt

1¾ cups plus 2 tablespoons (227 grams) all-purpose flour, sifted

The technique used to make this shortbread is unusual, but it yields incredibly tender, melt-in-your-mouth cookies. Made with half melted butter (which prevents the shortbread from spreading) and half softened butter (which lightens the texture), this elegant, sophisticated shortbread is simple to make and keeps well. Steeping a small amount of toasted caraway seeds in the melted butter infuses the shortbread with a unique perfume. Make sure your melted butter has cooled completely before you whisk in the soft butter, or it will all melt!

1. Put the caraway seeds in a medium saucepan and lightly toast over medium heat just until you wake up their aroma, about a minute. Remove the pan from the heat, then add 8 tablespoons (113.5 grams) of the butter. Return the pan to low heat and melt the butter. Remove the pan from the heat, cover, and set aside in a warm place to steep for an hour.

2. Combine the sugar and salt in a wide glass or stainless steel bowl. Add the caraway-infused butter, whisking furiously; the mixture will emulsify, resembling mayonnaise. Check to make sure the butter is completely cool, then whisk in the remaining 8 tablespoons (113.5 grams) soft butter until homogeneous and smooth. Dump in all the flour at once and, using your hand like a claw, rake through the dough until the flour is fully incorporated and the dough is homogeneous. This should be fun, and not much work.

3. Transfer the dough to a sheet of parchment, waxed paper, or plastic wrap and form into a 4¼-by-6-inch (11-by-15-centimeter) block. Chill the dough for at least a few hours, or up to overnight, until very firm.

4. Preheat the oven to 300°F (150°C). Line two sheet pans with parchment or silicone baking mats.

5. With a sharp knife, slice the chilled dough crosswise into rectangles ¼ inch (0.5 centimeter) thick. Arrange the cookies on the prepared pans, spacing them about ¾ inch (2 centimeters) apart. Give each cookie a fairy dusting of sugar and bake for 20 minutes, or until browned on the edges, with some golden-blond coloring all over. Remove from the oven and let cool on the pans. The cookies will keep in an airtight container for up to 1 week.

BROWN BUTTER–TOFFEE SHORTBREAD

Pictured on page 213

Makes about 2 dozen cookies

½ pound (227 grams) unsalted butter, very soft

⅓ cup (62 grams) light Muscovado sugar (see page 21)

¾ teaspoon kosher salt

1¾ cups plus 2 tablespoons (227 grams) all-purpose flour, sifted

¼ cup (15 grams) finely chopped toffee, homemade (page 235) or store-bought

As with the Caraway Seed Shortbread (opposite), these cookies are made with a combination of melted and soft butter, but here the melted butter is browned, which gives the cookies a wonderful toasty, nutty flavor.

1. Melt 8 tablespoons (113.5 grams) of the butter in a medium saucepan over medium heat, whisking occasionally. Meanwhile, set a heatproof bowl over a bowl of ice and keep near the stove. When the butter begins to foam, whisk it vigorously, making sure you get into the bottom and corners of the pan so that it doesn't burn. When it starts to brown and smells like toasted hazelnuts, remove from the heat and immediately pour it into the bowl set over the ice. If it seems like the heat is carrying over and the butter is still getting darker, keep whisking with all your heart until enough heat is released to stop the cooking. Then pull the bowl off the ice; you aren't trying to chill it, just keep it from overbrowning. Let cool until lukewarm.

2. Add the sugar and salt to the lukewarm butter and whisk together until very smooth and incorporated, then whisk in the remaining 8 tablespoons (113.5 grams) soft butter. Dump in the flour and toffee bits and use your hand like a claw to incorporate the flour into the butter-sugar mixture. Turn the dough out onto a sheet of parchment and pat into a 4¼-by-6-inch (11-by-15-centimeter) rectangle. Chill for 20 minutes. (*The dough can be refrigerated for up to 2 days or frozen for up to a month. Once it is cold, wrap tightly in plastic wrap for storage. If you chill the dough for longer than 20 minutes, be sure to let it soften at room temperature before slicing, or it will be very brittle and difficult to slice cleanly.*)

3. Preheat the oven to 300°F (150°C). Line two sheet pans with parchment.

4. Remove the dough from the refrigerator (if it has been refrigerated for more than 20 minutes, you'll need to let it warm slightly before slicing). With a sharp knife, slice the dough into rectangles ¼ inch (0.5 centimeter) thick. Transfer to the prepared sheet pans, spacing them about 1 inch (2.5 centimeters) apart.

5. Bake for 20 to 24 minutes, until the cookies look set; don't judge by color, because the raw dough is already quite brown. Transfer to wire racks and let cool completely. The cookies will keep in an airtight container for up to 1 week.

From left to right: Bulgarian Shortbread (page 217);
Plum Kiffels (page 221); Caraway Seed Shortbread
(208); Cacao Nib Sandwich Cookies (page 229);
Brown Butter–Toffee Shortbread (209)

VANILLA KIPFERL
(Austrian Vanilla Crescent Cookies)

Makes about 40 cookies

1 vanilla bean, split lengthwise

¼ cup (50 grams) granulated sugar

½ pound (226 grams) unsalted butter, at room temperature

¾ teaspoon kosher salt

1⅔ cups (199 grams) all-purpose flour

1 cup plus 3 tablespoons (114 grams) almond meal (see page 17)

½ cup (57 grams) confectioners' sugar for rolling and dusting

For these crescent cookies, be sure to use the best almond meal you can find. Use natural (skin-on) almond meal. I love the taste of the whole almond in desserts, and once you start using the whole meal, I think you'll find the blanched kind to be missing something.

To make the work of shaping these cookies more efficient, you first shape the dough into long, skinny logs while it is still very soft, then chill it. When you are ready to shape the cookies, cut the dough into equal pieces and let them warm slightly, then taper the ends of each and carefully bend into a crescent.

1. Preheat the oven to 325°F (165°C). Line two sheet pans with parchment.

2. Place the vanilla bean and granulated sugar in the bowl of a stand mixer (or a large bowl) and, using your fingers, rub and scrape the bean with the sugar to exfoliate every bit of vanilla goodness from your pod. Remove the used pod from the sugar but save it—it can be infused in your favorite spirit or dropped into a container of granulated sugar to make vanilla-scented sugar.

3. Add the butter and salt to the sugar, transfer the bowl to the mixer stand, fitted with the paddle attachment (or use a handheld mixer), and cream on medium-high speed until very light in color and fluffy, 3 to 4 minutes. Whisk together the flour and almond meal and add to the butter in 3 additions, mixing after each addition until almost combined. Remove the bowl from the stand (if using a stand mixer) and finish incorporating the last addition of flour by hand; the dough should be homogeneous.

4. Divide the dough into 5 equal pieces (4 ounces/113 grams each). Working with one piece at a time, roll the dough into 10-inch (46-centimeter) logs, then chill for at least 20 minutes. (*The logs of dough can be wrapped in plastic wrap and refrigerated for up to a week.*)

5. When you're ready to shape the cookies, cut the logs into 2-inch (5-centimeter) pieces. Taper the ends of each piece, bend into a crescent shape, and place on one of the prepared pans, leaving at least ¾ inch (2 centimeters) between the cookies.

(continued)

POPPY SEED RUGELACH

Makes 32 cookies

½ pound (227 grams) unsalted butter, soft but still cool

8 ounces (227 grams) cream cheese (see headnote), at room temperature

¼ cup (50 grams) granulated sugar

½ teaspoon kosher salt

1½ cups (180 grams) all-purpose flour

1½ cups (456 grams) Poppy Seed Filling (page 147)

1 large egg, beaten, for egg wash

Demerara sugar (see page 21) for sprinkling

Of all the Ashkenazi Jewish foods out there, none is as well-known as rugelach, a filled, rolled cookie that you can find at every Jewish bakery and bar/bat mitzvah celebration the world over. It likely first gained notoriety in the United States when a recipe was included in a 1950s cookbook at the same time cream cheese was becoming a more widely available ingredient.

You'll notice that this dough has equal parts cream cheese and butter and less flour than either of them, but it really works! I like to use a natural cream cheese without stabilizers, which is why I don't cream the cheese with the butter, but if you're using Philadelphia cream cheese, or another brand that contains stabilizers, add it at the same time as the butter.

This dough is made like puff pastry. You roll it, fold it, and let it chill, then repeat the process two more times. It's a bit fiddly, but it gives the finished dough many flaky layers. I like to use a poppy seed filling for these cookies, but you could substitute jam, Sour Cherry Lekvar (page 38) or Plum Lekvar (page 77), or the Walnut Filling (page 147).

1. In the bowl of a stand mixer fitted with the paddle attachment (or in a large bowl, using a handheld mixer), cream the butter (if you're using a cream cheese with stabilizers added, such as Philadelphia, add it along with the butter), granulated sugar, and salt on medium-high speed until fluffy. If using a natural (stabilizer-free) cream cheese, crumble it in and mix on low speed until just incorporated; be careful not to overmix. Add the flour and pulse the mixer off and on until the flour is incorporated.

2. Transfer the mixture to a sheet of plastic wrap and use the plastic to help shape the dough into a rectangle. Wrap tightly and refrigerate until cold, at least 2 hours, or up to overnight.

3. On a lightly floured work surface, with a lightly floured rolling pin, roll the dough into a rectangle that is approximately 10 by 15 inches (25 by 38 centimeters), with a short end toward you. Use a dry pastry brush to brush off any excess flour. Fold the top third of the dough down over the center, brushing off the excess flour, then fold the bottom third of the dough over, as you would fold a business letter. Rotate the dough 90 degrees counterclockwise so that the open seam is on the right. This is the first turn. The packet of dough should be 5 inches (12 centimeters) wide by 10 inches (25 centimeters) long.

(continued)

STRUDEL

Strudel is magic. If you really want to capture the attention of a room and hold the occupants in your hand, or, I should say, on the backs of your hands, start stretching a strudel dough in the middle of a full house. I've had to scold customers who tried putting their dirty dishes on top of my dough ("I thought it was just a tablecloth!"), and I've played it cool while my dough was tearing, scrambling to get it rolled up before the overhanging piece tumbled to the floor.

You may ask why I put myself through such torture, and I will tell you: Because making strudel is fun. Fun like a roller coaster without seat belts, but so, so fun.

Of all the traditional Viennese pastries, strudel is the most challenging to master but certainly the most rewarding. When you descend the stairs to the lowest floor of Demel, the legendary *Konditorei* in Vienna, you will find a beautiful glassed-in production room where you can see cakes being finished, chocolate being poured into molds, and, of course, strudel being stretched and pulled, buttered, and filled. Visually, a finished strudel might not impress people the same way as a Honey Cake (page 151) will (part of the reason I think it's a good time to show off this technique in my restaurant), but so much of what we bake is a gift for others, and the validation we receive is external.

Make strudel because you love baking and you love a challenge, and I promise that the elation you feel when your strudel succeeds will exceed any sense of accomplishment you've experienced previously in the kitchen. No matter the state of your kitchen, or how much flour may be in your hair, imagine you are in that room at Demel, surrounded by mahogany tables covered with marble, stretching a flawless dough so thin you can read a newspaper through it. Bah! Yours will be thinner!

Using the right flour will make this dough beautiful and easy to manage. I have used both 14% protein and 12.5% protein flours in this recipe, and the 14% never failed. You can still make the dough if you can't find exactly the right high-gluten bread flour, but it will be a little more fragile and less pliable. I imagine you might be asking yourself, "But won't this high-gluten flour result in a tough dough that is not magic to eat?" No, I say! The apple cider vinegar in the recipe relaxes the dough, and all the butter that is carefully spread on each layer makes a wonderfully crispy, flaky, and delicate pastry.

Skills and Equipment

This chapter's recipes require the most skill but the least equipment. I implore you to use a kitchen scale for this project, even for the volume measurements. This stern warning comes from a person who loves to wing it and who throws caution to the wind on a regular basis; I do not mess with strudel dough. Play with the fillings all you want—from kasha and cabbage to chocolate and nuts. Or wild nettles, wild mushrooms, apples, peaches, or farmer's cheese. Sweet or savory, there's a strudel for every season. You may need to adjust the filling amount depending on the size of your table; please make notations right in your book! (I know it's hard to write in books, but it's okay. You will be a better baker for it.) You will also need a lint-free tablecloth or a sheet that is larger than your table and a pastry brush.

The Strudel Manifesto: Making and Stretching the Dough

Next to becoming one with the dough while stretching it, the most important part of successful strudel making lies in the mixing, kneading, and resting of the dough.

There are no guarantees in life, or in strudel-making, but there is preparedness! If you're anything like me, knowing it's okay to mess up will make you a hundred times less likely to do so: Do what I do, and make a double batch of dough as an insurance policy. Just before your last knead, divide the dough in two, then proceed with one portion as for the single batch. If you mess up the first one, you've got a backup. And if you don't screw up, you can freeze the extra dough in an airtight container for your next strudel adventure.

This recipe requires time, space, and patience. You'll need a large freestanding surface on which you can stretch the dough, ideally a rectangular or square table. Because you need to stretch the dough from all sides, a countertop won't do. You'll also need a tablecloth to assist you in rolling the dough.

3 cups (358 grams) organic high-gluten flour (14 to 15%; if using a bread flour with a lower percentage of protein, add an extra kneading cycle to the dough)

¾ teaspoon kosher salt

⅛ teaspoon baking powder

½ cup plus 1 tablespoon (112 grams) grapeseed or canola oil, plus more for coating the dough

1 large egg

1 large egg yolk

10½ tablespoons (150 grams) warm (body-temperature) water

1¼ teaspoons apple cider vinegar

1. In a medium bowl, whisk together the flour, salt, and baking powder, then create a well in the center. In a small bowl, whisk together the oil, egg, and egg yolk until it emulsifies a little (like you're making salad dressing). Whisk in the water and vinegar, then pour the mixture into the well in the dry ingredients. Using your hand like a claw, starting in the middle, stir the ingredients together, gradually pulling in and moistening the dry ingredients until you have a homogeneous dough. It will not look supersmooth, but it should be evenly mixed, with absolutely no dry spots.

(continued)

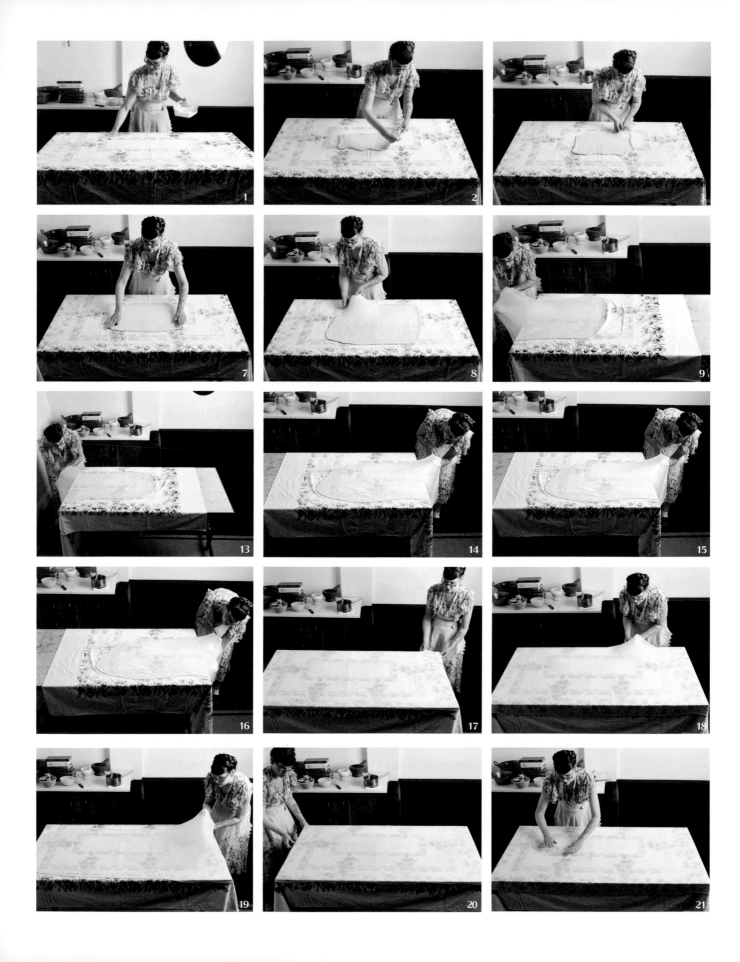

10. Once you can pull the dough over all four corners of the table, use a pastry brush to splatter it all over with the butter-oil mixture, and use your hands to pat and brush the butter evenly over the dough. I call this move "Jackson Pollock Strudel Bongos." The corners of the table will become your ideal strudel stretching partner; you can trust them implicitly to hold the dough in place while you attend to your buttering duties. If you feel as if you can get more stretch out of the dough, I suggest you keep going. Then the overhang can be flipped over the filling, creating even more layers, or the strudel can be scooched up at the halfway point of rolling it up to continue adding layers with the extra dough. How do you know when to stop, you ask? When you've stretched your dough (and your nerves) to the breaking point! Using scissors, trim away the thick border of your stretched dough and discard it—be sure to trim the edges before proceeding; the dough is so thin that the weight of the thicker dough at the edges can actually cause the dough to tear along the entire edge of your table. This has happened to me! Take one deep breath (sorry, but this is not the time to let your dough dry out), and proceed with filling this beautiful sheet of dough.

APPLE STRUDEL

FOR ASSEMBLY

2 to 2½ pounds (908 grams to 1.135 kilograms) firm apples, depending on the size of your table

1 recipe strudel dough (see page 240)

All-purpose flour for dusting

⅔ cup (158 milliliters) melted clarified butter (recipe follows)

2 tablespoons (30 milliliters) grapeseed oil

3 tablespoons (36 grams) sugar

6 tablespoons (42 grams) dry cookie, cake, or bread crumbs (see Crumbs, page 35)

Pinch of kosher salt

Whipped Cream (page 330) for serving

It's tough to beat the smell of a freshly baked apple dessert emerging from the oven on a chilly day. And when we think of strudel, it's apple that comes to mind for most of us.

I'm devoted to farmer Stan Devoto; his are the apples of my eye. Pink Pearl, Burgundy, Sierra Beauty, Belle de Boskoop, Arkansas Black, and Black Twig are some of my favorites. Part of what I look for in a strudel apple is flavor, of course, but whatever kind of person you are—sweet, tart, spicy, or tannic—a hard, dense-fleshed apple is going to bake up the best, and these are all terrific examples. If you can't get to a farmers' market, and you don't have a fancy grocery store nearby, something like a Pippin, which is drier than, say, a Granny Smith, would be a good choice. If your fruit is on the juicier side, add extra crumbs both under the fruit and 6 inches (15 centimeters) beyond where the fruit is to prevent the strudel from becoming soggy.

I like to keep it simple when it comes to fruit in desserts, so in this strudel, I let the apple star; you'll notice that there isn't any cinnamon or other spice to meddle with its perfect fragrance. But I won't judge you for sneaking in some cinnamon, candied ginger, huckleberries, or lemon.

1. **PREPARE THE FRUIT:** Shortly before you're ready to stretch your strudel dough, peel the apples and use a melon baller to remove the blossom and stem ends. (I give a weight range for the apples because you might need more or less depending on the size of the table you're using to stretch the dough.) Halve each apple and use the melon baller to remove the core from each half. Slice each apple half crosswise into ⅛-inch (0.3-centimeter) slices, then press the slices back together so they look like an apple half again. Set aside. (*This can be done a couple of hours ahead. Don't worry about needing lemon juice to prevent the apples from browning; using a crisp high-acid variety helps keep them from oxidizing more than lemon juice would, and you won't notice any browning after the strudel is baked.*)

2. Preheat the oven to 375°F (190°C).

3. Stretch and butter the dough according to the instructions in The Strudel Manifesto (see page 243), using the clarified butter and grapeseed oil.

4. Lightly sprinkle the dough with a fairy dusting of the sugar and crumbs. Then, on one of the short sides, very close to the edge, sprinkle a heavier

layer of crumbs in a straight band about 4 inches (10 centimeters) wide. Lay the sliced apples down in a line on top of the crumbs. You don't want to really fan the apple slices out; just pop them open slightly. Brush the tops of the apples with some of the butter-oil mixture and sprinkle with a fairy dusting of sugar and the pinch of salt.

5. Now, standing at the short side of your table and using the tablecloth as your assistant, flip the overhanging dough up and over the apples, enclosing them in a single layer of dough (if you don't have any overhang on this side, that's okay; you can basically just flip the apples over to enclose them in dough). Brush the dough that you just flipped over the apples with a bit of the butter-oil mixture. Continuing to use the tablecloth as your assistant, roll the strudel halfway down the length of the table, enclosing the apples in the buttery dough.

6. When you've rolled about halfway down the length of the table, use the tablecloth to pull the whole thing toward you, then continue rolling until you reach the end (for god's sake, don't flip it onto the floor!). You can karate-chop a dent in the middle of your roll to make 2 strudels, or keep it whole and make a large round strudel. For a large round strudel, insert one open end inside the other after trimming the thick unfilled dough away from each end, so the strudel looks like a snake eating its own tail. This will make a beautiful wreath-shaped strudel that won't blow out on the ends while baking. For 2 strudels, keep karate-chopping and pressing to scooch your filling away from the dent, then cut the strudel in half, fold each cut part under, and pinch to seal. If the filling is coming out of the dough, gently stretch to pinch the dough together first, then fold under and pinch again.

7. Line a sheet pan with parchment and lightly brush with some of the butter-oil mixture. Carefully lay your strudel baby (or babies) on the prepared pan and brush the entire surface with more of the butter-oil mixture. The strudel can be baked immediately, or you can chill it on the pan until the butter you brushed on the exterior is firm, then wrap the pan tightly with plastic wrap and refrigerate until ready to bake. (*The assembled strudel can be refrigerated for up to 3 days.*)

DRIED PLUM, HAZELNUT, AND CHOCOLATE STRUDEL

FOR THE FILLING

1 pound (454 grams) dried plums (see page 18) or 1¼ pounds (568 grams) pitted prunes, sliced about ¼ inch (0.5 centimeter) thick

1 cup (237 milliliters) water (see headnote)

½ cup (99 grams) sugar (see headnote)

1½ cups (200 grams) hazelnuts

4 ounces (113 grams) bittersweet chocolate (65% to 78% cacao), chopped

2 tablespoons (22 grams) chopped candied citron or ginger (optional)

Pinch of kosher salt

FOR ASSEMBLY

1 recipe strudel dough (see page 240)

⅔ cup (158 milliliters) melted clarified butter (page 250)

2 tablespoons (30 milliliters) grapeseed oil

2 tablespoons (24 grams) sugar for sprinkling

Vanilla Sauce (page 338), spiked with Armagnac or nocino (walnut liqueur), if desired, or Whipped Cream (page 330) for serving

Even here in California, the land of practically year-round fresh produce, there are some notable gaps. But nuts, chocolate, and delicious dried fruit do a splendid job of filling in the cracks between apple and rhubarb season. Reminiscent of fruitcake (in a good way!), this strudel makes a perfect dessert for Christmas dinner or pastry for Christmas morning.

The dried plums I use here are pretty dry, like leather, and very tart. If you're using prunes instead, omit the sugar and water, and look for fruit that is moist and plump and yields to the gentle pressure of a sharp knife. Even though you can plump the plums and then make the strudel the same day, the plums really do improve with a day of soaking, so I strongly recommend it. I use raw hazelnuts here instead of bread crumbs as in the other strudel recipes, since the dried fruit doesn't need the crumbs to soak up the liquid. You couldn't go wrong with a healthy splash of Armagnac or nocino on the plums!

1. **MAKE THE FILLING:** Put the plums in a bowl, add the water, and mix in the sugar—really work the sugar and water into the plums for a few minutes. Cover and set aside to plump for at least 3 hours, but preferably overnight.

2. Grind the hazelnuts in a food processor or finely chop them; set aside.

3. **ASSEMBLE AND BAKE THE STRUDEL:** Preheat the oven to 375°F (190°C).

4. Stretch and butter the strudel dough according to The Strudel Manifesto (see page 243), using the clarified butter and grapeseed oil.

5. Lightly sprinkle the dough with a fairy dusting of the sugar and hazelnuts. On one of the long sides, very close to the edge, sprinkle a heavier layer of hazelnuts in a straight band about 3 inches (8 centimeters) wide. Lay the macerated plums down in a line on top of the nuts. Scatter the chocolate over the plums and then the chopped citron, if using. Sprinkle a fairy dusting of sugar over the filling and all over the dough and sprinkle the pinch of salt over the band of filling.

6. Now, standing at the long side of your table and using the tablecloth as your assistant, flip the overhanging dough up and over the plums, enclosing them in a single layer of dough (if you don't have any overhang on this side, that's okay; you'll basically just be flipping the plums over to

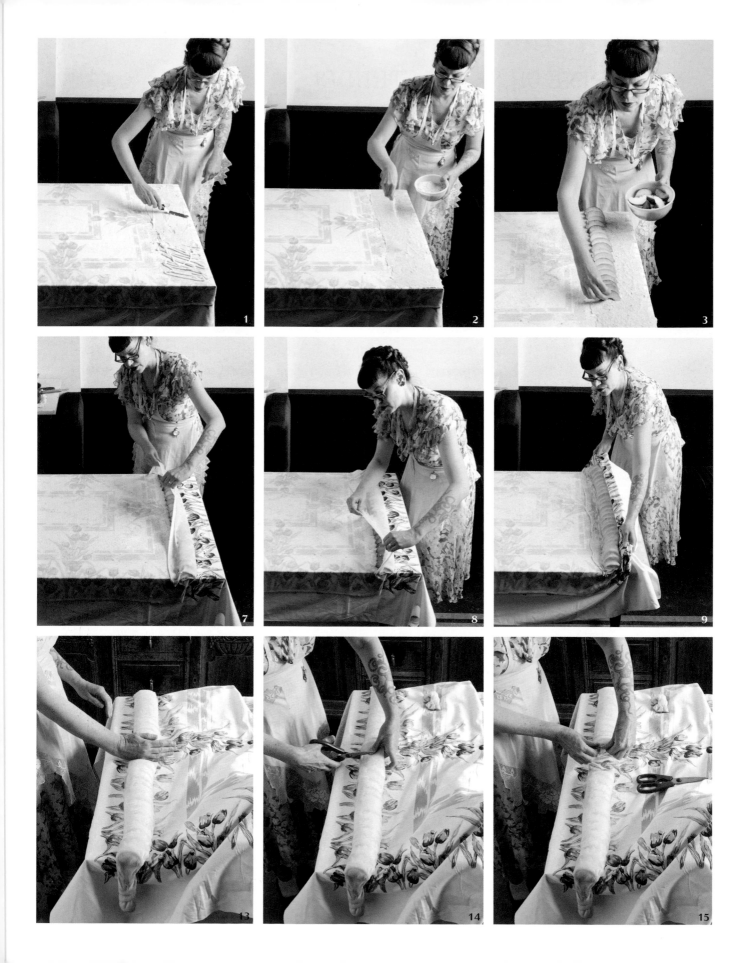

7. Standing at the long side of your table and using the tablecloth as your assistant, flip the overhanging dough up and over the band of filling, enclosing it in a single layer of dough (if you don't have any overhang on this side, that's okay; you'll basically just be rolling the filling over to enclose it in dough. Brush the dough you've just flipped over with a bit of the butter-oil mix. Continuing to use the cloth as your assistant, roll the pastry halfway down the width of the table.

8. When you've rolled about halfway down the width of the table, use the tablecloth to pull the whole thing toward you, then continue rolling until you reach the end (for god's sake, don't flip it onto the floor!). Pinch each end closed. Beginning at one end, spiral the strudel into a pinwheel, twisting the roll as you spiral it to create lovely pleats (or wrinkles) on the surface of the dough, thereby creating more surface area and extra crunch in the finished pastry. Pinch the outer end again and tuck it under the pastry so it stays put while baking. Carefully transfer the pinwheel to the prepared pan and brush the whole thing with the butter-oil mix, getting inside the spiral to the parts where the dough touches itself. (*The assembled pie can be refrigerated for up to 2 days before baking.*)

9. Brush the pinwheel all over with the egg wash and sprinkle with sea salt if desired. With the tip of a sharp knife, cut a few steam vents in the top at regular intervals. Bake until the pie is golden brown, 35 to 45 minutes.

10. Serve the pie warm, cut into wedges, or cool completely and pack it up for a picnic!

SAVORY
PASTRIES

CHEDDAR-BACON POGÁCSA
(Hungarian Savory Scones)

Makes 18 pogácsa

4¾ cups (570 grams) all-purpose flour

2 tablespoons (35 grams) baking powder

2¼ teaspoons kosher salt

½ teaspoon mildly spicy chile flakes, such as Aleppo (optional)

1 cup (237 milliliters) heavy cream

1 tablespoon crumbled fresh (cake) yeast or 1 teaspoon instant dry yeast

1 cup plus 1 tablespoon (241 grams) sour cream

1 cup (113 grams) grated cheddar cheese (about 4 ounces)

¼ cup (10 grams) finely chopped chives

4 to 6 slices bacon, cooked and finely chopped

½ pound (226 grams) cold unsalted butter, cut into small cubes

1 egg, beaten, for egg wash

Flaky sea salt, such as Maldon, or nigella seeds or poppy seeds (see page 20) for sprinkling

This delicious yeasted "biscuit" is unique to Hungary, although similar pastries with similar names can be found all over the Balkans and the Carpathian Basin. Every Hungarian I have met has their own recipe for these, and they are usually a source of great family pride. The pastry may look like a cross between a scone and a biscuit, but these delightful morsels are so much more. They are leavened three ways—with yeast, lamination, and baking powder—to achieve a flakiness and prevent a heaviness that could otherwise be a pitfall with so many fatty ingredients wedged into one dough.

The addition of baking powder is not traditional, but it gives the dough a little extra lift. A trick I recently learned for laminating, or putting turns in the dough (as for croissant and puff pastry), is to actually cut the dough and stack it to create the turns, rather than folding it, which is the way I was taught, and what I had practiced for more than twenty-five years. This new technique makes for a much clearer delineation of layers, and you won't end up with those wonky ones that happen in the folded parts of the dough.

Even though there is a ton of fat in this dough, the liquid from the cream and sour cream can still make it tough if you don't respect the gluten and give the dough the proper time to rest between turns. If while rolling you feel it resist or spring back in any way, drop your weapon (I mean rolling pin), wrap up the dough, and chill it for 30 minutes before touching it again.

I like to make tiny pogácsa to serve as a snack with wine and larger ones as a morning or afternoon pastry. This is another recipe with interchangeable parts, so feel free to be creative, swapping out different cheeses or herbs for the ones suggested here, keeping your proportions in line with the ones listed, and make your own legendary family recipe!

1. Combine the flour, baking powder, salt, chile flakes, if using, in a large bowl and set aside. Pour the cream into a medium bowl and add the yeast to the cream. Add the sour cream, whisk to combine, and set aside.

2. Add the cheese, chives, and bacon to the dry ingredients and stir to combine, coating the ingredients in flour. Add the cubed butter and work it into the flour with a pastry blender or your fingers. Some butter pieces should be the size of peas, but some larger pieces are okay. Make a well in the center of the mixture and pour in the wet ingredients. Use your hand

like a claw to pull the dried ingredients into the creamy center and rake everything around, distributing the wet and dry bits evenly, until no dry or wet spots remain. Transfer the dough to a sheet of plastic wrap and pat into a rectangle that is 1½ inches (4 centimeters) thick. Wrap in the plastic, and chill for 1 hour.

3. On a floured work surface, with a floured rolling pin, roll the dough into a rectangle that is 13 by 24 inches (33 by 60 centimeters). Use a dry pastry brush to brush off any excess flour. Cut the dough into three 8-by-13-inch (20-by-33-centimeter) rectangles, meticulously brushing off the excess flour. Stack the rectangles of dough on top of one another, then turn the stack so a short side is in front of your belly. This is the first "turn." Roll the dough to an 8-by-18 inch (20-by-45-centimeter) rectangle, wrap in plastic, and chill for 30 to 45 minutes, until cold and firm.

4. Repeat the rolling, cutting, and stacking process two more times for a total of 3 turns, chilling after each turn.

5. When ready to roll and cut the pogácsa, preheat the oven to 375°F (190°C). Line two sheet pans with parchment.

6. On a lightly floured work surface, with a lightly floured rolling pin, roll the dough to a thickness of ¾ inch (2 centimeters). Using a sharp paring knife, score the dough diagonally in one direction, then again in the opposite direction to create a diamond pattern, cutting no deeper than ⅛ inch (0.3 centimeter).

7. Using a 2¾-inch (7-centimeter) round cutter, cut out the pogácsa and place on the prepared pans, spacing them about 2 inches (5 centimeters) apart. (The scraps can be gathered together, chilled or frozen, and rerolled once.) (*The pogácsa can be made ahead and frozen before baking. Freeze in a single layer on a sheet pan until frozen solid, then transfer to a freezer bag and freeze for up to 2 months. They can be baked from frozen; just add a few minutes to the baking time.*)

8. Brush the pogácsa with the beaten egg and sprinkle with flaky salt. Transfer to the oven and bake until puffed and golden brown, about 30 minutes. Serve warm or at room temperature.

(continued)

Feta-Herb Pogácsa

Omit the bacon and replace the cheddar with 1 cup (220 grams) crumbled feta (if it's stored in brine, dry it with paper towels before crumbling). Instead of the chives, use ½ cup (42 grams) finely chopped soft herbs—chives could make up a portion, but you can also add chervil, parsley, dill, tarragon, or whatever else you have on hand.

CHEF POLZINSKI'S PIEROGI

Makes 30 dumplings;
serves 6

FOR THE DOUGH

2 cups (240 grams) all-purpose flour, plus more for dusting

½ teaspoon baking powder

½ teaspoon kosher salt

½ cup (114 grams) sour cream

2 large eggs

FOR THE FILLING

1 pound (454 grams) Yukon Gold potatoes, peeled, halved if small, quartered if large

Kosher salt

1½ tablespoons extra-virgin olive oil

1½ tablespoons (21 grams) unsalted butter

1 medium white or yellow onion, thinly sliced from stem to root

½ teaspoon ground coriander

¼ teaspoon ground yellow mustard seeds or dry mustard

¼ teaspoon caraway seeds

Pinch of red chile flakes

1 tiny garlic clove (one of those little ones from the middle of the head that you usually hate), minced

Who doesn't love a dumpling? I'm talking about dumplings of delicious dough, whether crispy, pillowy, or chewy, filled with the treasure of a well-seasoned filling. So many cultures can boast of extraordinary dumplings: Japanese gyoza, Chinese xiao long bao, Italian ravioli. Central Europe has a whole host of sweet dumplings. These particular dumplings hail from Poland, the land of my people (or so I've been told).

The dough is made of sour cream, eggs, and flour, and when the pierogi are boiled and then panfried with butter and poppy seeds, the result is at once crispy, chewy, and just a little bit pillowy—everything you could ask of a dumpling! The filling is nicely spiced, a little sweet and sour, and packed with umami from the sauerkraut, making these a very satisfying dish for vegetarians. Serve the pierogi with a spoonful of Damson Plum Preserves (page 80) or sour cherry preserves and sour cream.

Pierogi take a little time to make, but they can be made ahead and frozen after boiling and shocking. They don't need to be oiled to keep them from sticking together, but do let the surface get nice and dry before freezing. Because the potato filling is dense, they should be thawed overnight in the refrigerator before panfrying.

1. **MAKE THE DOUGH:** Stir together the flour, baking powder, and salt in a medium bowl and make a well in the center. Add the sour cream to the well and crack the eggs on top. Using your hand like a claw, stir the sour cream and eggs together, then gradually pull the dry ingredients into the center until you have a nice dough. Scrape out onto a lightly floured counter and knead a few times until everything is homogeneous. Cover the dough so it doesn't dry out (I use an inverted bowl) and let it rest for 10 minutes.

2. When you return to the dough, you'll notice how remarkably smooth and stretchy it has become! Give it a few more kneads, then let rest, covered, for 10 more minutes. Knead again, cover, and rest the dough for 30 minutes. Then refrigerate the dough, covered, until ready to use, or wrap tightly and freeze. (*The dough can be frozen for up to 1 month. Thaw overnight in the refrigerator.*)

3. **MAKE THE FILLING:** Put the potatoes in a medium saucepan and add water to cover by a few inches (about 8 centimeters). Generously salt the water,

(continued)

¼ cup plus 2 tablespoons (60 grams) sauerkraut (squeezed to remove the liquid before measuring)

6 ounces (170 grams) farmer's cheese or old-fashioned (i.e., stabilizer-free) cream cheese

Freshly ground black pepper

FOR SERVING

6 tablespoons (85 grams) unsalted butter

3 tablespoons (45 milliliters) grapeseed or canola oil

2 teaspoons poppy seeds (see page 20)

Sour cream

Damson Plum Preserves (page 80) or sour cherry preserves

bring to a boil over high heat, and cook until the potatoes are tender, about 10 minutes. Drain the potatoes and mash with a potato masher. Set aside.

4. In a medium frying pan, heat the olive oil and butter over low heat. When the butter has melted and stopped foaming, add the onion, spices, and a few fat pinches of salt and cook, stirring occasionally, until the onion is soft and starting to caramelize, about 20 minutes. Add the garlic and cook for another couple of minutes, until you can no longer taste raw garlic. Remove from the heat and stir in the sauerkraut, then turn the mixture out onto a cutting board and chop pretty small (but don't lose your mind here). Transfer to a bowl, stir in the mashed potatoes and farmer's cheese, and season to taste with salt and pepper. Let cool completely.

5. Once the filling is cool, use two teaspoons to form the mixture into 30 quenelles (i.e., resembling small footballs) and set on a sheet pan lined with parchment.

6. **TO ASSEMBLE THE PIEROGI:** Put a clean, dry tea towel on a sheet pan and lightly dust it with flour. On a lightly floured work surface, with a lightly floured rolling pin, roll the dough out very evenly to about ⅛ inch. Cover the dough with plastic wrap and let rest for 10 minutes.

7. Using a 4-inch (10-centimeter) round cutter, stamp out as many rounds as you can from the dough, leaving them in place. Pull away the scraps, gather into a ball, and knead a few times; set aside.

8. Place one quenelle of filling in the center of each dough circle. Using a bench scraper to aid you (the dough is sticky and delicate!), lift one edge of a round of dough up and over the filling, aligning the edges. Press the dough to seal, then use the bench scraper to lift the dumpling from the table, starting from the folded side; recheck the seal and set the dumpling seam side up on the flour-dusted tea towel. Repeat with the remaining circles of dough. Reroll the scraps of dough and stamp out more dough circles (you should have 30 in total) and repeat the filling and shaping; the rerolled dough will need to rest an additional 5 to 10 minutes to relax the gluten. Lightly cover the pan of assembled pierogi with plastic wrap and chill for at least 30 minutes, or up to 2 hours.

(continued)

9. Bring a large pot of salted water to a boil. Fill a large bowl with ice and water. Remove the pierogi from the refrigerator. Using your index finger and thumb, pinch the edges of each one very well, thinning out the dough while creating a pretty ruffled edge and sealing in the filling forever; return to the tea towel.

10. Drop half of the pierogi into the boiling water. When they float to the surface, cook for 1 minute longer, then remove with a spider or slotted spoon and plunge into the ice bath. Once they are cool, remove from the ice bath and dry on a clean tea towel. Repeat with the remaining pierogi. (*The boiled pierogi can be refrigerated in an airtight container for up to 2 days. Or you can freeze the boiled pierogi: Arrange them on a parchment-lined sheet pan in a single layer and freeze until solid, then transfer to an airtight container and freeze for up to 2 months. Defrost in the refrigerator overnight before panfrying.*)

11. When you are ready to serve, combine the butter and oil in a large frying pan and heat over medium heat. When the butter stops foaming, add half of the pierogi and panfry, turning as needed, until golden brown and puffy all over, especially on that ruffle! Transfer to a serving platter and repeat with the remaining pierogi. Sprinkle with the poppy seeds and serve immediately, with sour cream and Damson plum or sour cherry preserves alongside.

SAVORY TARTLETS

Though I call these tartlets, they aren't as fiddly as the name might suggest. Rather than forming individual bite-size tarts (a royal pain), you bake the dough as a single large sheet and then top it and cut it into rectangles. These make a great hors d'oeuvre, but if you cut them into larger pieces, you could serve them as lunch or a light supper with a salad alongside. As with the Rustic Tarts (page 299), you can top these tartlets with whatever your heart desires, although I'm giving you two favorite combinations. And here's a third, easy idea: Bake the dough as directed, then spread with a thin layer of stone fruit or fig preserves and top with arugula or watercress and shavings of Pecorino Romano or Parmesan cheese.

15 spears asparagus, ends trimmed and cut into 2-inch (5-centimeter) lengths

2½ tablespoons (37 milliliters) olive oil

1 tablespoon (14 grams) unsalted butter, melted

Meyer Lemon Relish (recipe follows) for serving

rope-shaped edge. Sprinkle the tart with the remaining Parmesan, then brush the crust with the melted butter.

5. Bake the tart on the lowest oven rack until the crust is golden brown and the top is pocked with brown spots, 30 to 35 minutes. Remove from the oven and slide the tart (still on its parchment) onto a cooling rack. Let cool until warm or room temperature.

6. Serve the tart sliced into wedges, drizzled with the Meyer Lemon Relish.

Meyer Lemon Relish

Makes about ½ cup (118 milliliters)

1 small shallot, minced

2 tablespoons (30 milliliters) champagne vinegar

½ teaspoon honey

1 Meyer lemon, halved, seeded, and very finely chopped (rind and all!)

2 teaspoons kosher salt

2 tablespoons (30 milliliters) extra-virgin olive oil

This bright, fragrant relish boosts the flavor of the asparagus tart. Note that because it uses the whole lemon (peel and all), it can only be made with thin-skinned Meyer lemons.

1. In a small bowl, stir together the minced shallot, vinegar, and honey. In a second small bowl, combine the finely chopped lemon and salt. Let stand (separately) for 1 hour.

2. Stir the lemon into the shallot mixture. Stir in the olive oil. The relish will keep, refrigerated, for a few days. Let come to room temperature before serving.

Gypsy Pepper, Feta, and Tomato Tart

Makes one 12-inch (30.5-centimeter) tart; serves 4 to 6

1 recipe Crunch Dough (page 36)

2 tablespoons (30 milliliters) extra-virgin olive oil

1 or 2 Gypsy pepper (or other thin-skinned mild pepper), seeded and thinly sliced

Kosher salt

½ cup (113 grams) crème fraîche, homemade (page 337) or store-bought

1 large egg yolk

Freshly ground black pepper

1 cup (138 grams) cherry tomatoes, halved

3 scallions, white and light green parts only, cut into 1½-inch (4-centimeter) lengths

½ cup (76 grams) crumbled feta cheese

1 tablespoon (14 grams) unsalted butter, melted

A generous handful of packed soft herb leaves, such as parsley, chervil, chives, cilantro, or dill, or a mixture

Make this tart in deep summer, when you can find thin-skinned peppers at the farmers' market. For thicker-skinned varieties, char the skin over an open burner for a few minutes and peel before using.

1. On a lightly floured work surface, with a lightly floured rolling pin, roll the dough into a 14-inch (35-centimeter) circle. Transfer to a sheet of parchment, set on a round pizza pan or a sheet pan, and refrigerate for 20 minutes.

2. Position a rack in the lowest part of the oven and preheat the oven to 400°F (205°C).

3. In a nonstick frying pan, heat 1 tablespoon of the olive oil over medium heat. Add the sliced pepper(s) and a generous pinch of salt and cook, stirring, until the peppers have softened and are just beginning to brown, about 6 minutes. Remove from the heat and let cool slightly.

4. In a small bowl, stir together the crème fraîche and egg yolk and season with salt and pepper. In a second small bowl, toss the tomatoes and scallions with the remaining tablespoon of olive oil and season with a pinch of salt.

5. Remove the dough from the refrigerator and, with an offset spatula, spread the crème fraîche mixture over it in an even layer, leaving a ½-inch (1.5-centimeter) border all around. Spread the cooked peppers on top of the crème fraîche, then scatter the feta over. Top with the tomatoes and scallions, distributing them evenly over the tart. With a sharp knife or scissors, trim any ragged edges from the dough, then fold the edges of the tart over, twisting it loosely under itself and forming a rope-shaped edge. Brush the crust with the melted butter. (*The tart can be assembled up to an hour ahead and refrigerated until ready to bake.*)

6. Bake the tart on the lowest oven rack until the crust is golden brown and the top is pocked with brown spots, 30 to 35 minutes. Remove from the oven and slide the tart (still on its parchment) onto a cooling rack. Let cool until warm or at room temperature.

7. Just before serving, sprinkle the tart with the herbs, then slice into wedges.

GENTLEMAN'S TORTE
(Buckwheat and Herbed Cheese Crêpe Cake)

Serves 8

FOR THE CRÊPES

1⅓ cups (316 milliliters) whole milk

2 tablespoons (28 grams) unsalted butter, plus more for greasing the pan

¾ cup plus 1 tablespoon (200 grams) crème fraîche, homemade (page 337) or store-bought

2 large eggs

2 teaspoons crumbled fresh (cake) yeast or ¾ teaspoon instant dry yeast

1¼ teaspoons kosher salt

1 teaspoon sugar

1 cup (150 grams) buckwheat flour (see page 17)

Clarified butter (page 250) or grapeseed oil for cooking the crêpes

FOR THE FILLING

1 pound (454 grams) fresh goat cheese (chèvre), at room temperature

3 to 6 tablespoons (42 to 84 grams) sour cream

¼ to ½ teaspoon kosher salt, to taste

¼ to ½ teaspoon freshly ground black pepper, to taste

(continued)

I lifted the name "Gentleman's Torte" from an unrelated dish in an old Viennese cookbook. Much to my surprise, I recently discovered a similar savory Ukrainian crêpe cake called Pechinkoviy Torte.

I like using all buckwheat flour in the crêpe batter, both for flavor and for friends who can no longer eat wheat. The torte is layered with goat cheese and herbs; you can use any chopped herbs you like, but definitely add some chives to the mix. Serve the torte hot from the oven or slightly cooled; just be sure to serve it within an hour of baking to keep its lovely crispy edges. Be careful, though, as the layers can slide around a bit when the filling is hot.

1. **MAKE THE CRÊPES:** Combine the milk and butter in a small saucepan and heat over low heat, stirring, until the butter melts (do not let the mixture boil). Remove from the heat.

2. In a medium bowl, stir together the crème fraîche, eggs, yeast, salt, and sugar. Stir in the buckwheat flour until completely combined. Cover the bowl and set in a warm place for 30 minutes (I often set the bowl on top of the saucepan of warm milk), or until slightly puffed and a little bubbly. Whisk the milk mixture into the flour mixture.

3. Lightly grease an 8-inch (20-centimeter) crêpe pan or nonstick frying pan with clarified butter or grapeseed oil and heat over medium heat. When the pan is hot, lift it from the burner and ladle about 2 tablespoons (30 milliliters) of batter onto the center of the pan. Immediately tilt the pan in all directions to encourage the batter to coat the bottom in a thin, even layer. Return the pan to the burner and cook until the crêpe is lightly browned on one side (lift an edge to check), about 45 seconds. Use a small offset spatula to loosen the crêpe from the pan, then use a wide spatula to flip the crêpe (because these don't contain any gluten, they are more delicate than your average crêpe) and cook on the second side until browned, 30 to 45 seconds more. Transfer to a plate and repeat with the remaining batter, greasing the pan again as necessary to prevent the crêpes from sticking; you can stack the finished crêpes. You should end up with 18 crêpes.

(continued)

1¼ cups (84 to 126 grams) mixed chopped soft herbs, such as chives (essential!), parsley, thyme, and/or dill

FOR ASSEMBLY

6 tablespoons (85 grams) unsalted butter, melted

4. **MAKE THE FILLING:** In a medium bowl, stir together the goat cheese, 3 tablespoons (42 grams) of the sour cream, the salt, and pepper. The mixture should be spreadable but not loose; if you add too much sour cream, the filling will slide all over when you heat the cake. That said, the moisture content of goat cheese varies, so you may need to add some or all of the remaining 3 tablespoons (42 grams) sour cream to achieve a spreadable consistency.

5. **TO ASSEMBLE THE TORTE:** Find your prettiest crêpe and set it aside. Reserve a very small handful of the chopped herbs. Place one crêpe on an ovenproof plate, brush with melted butter, and then spread a heaping tablespoon of the filling evenly over it, leaving a ½- to ¾-inch (1.5- to 2-centimeter) border. Sprinkle with some of the chopped herbs, then top with a second crêpe. Continue the stacking until all the crêpes, filling, and herbs have been used. Lightly brush the top of the final crêpe with melted butter, then brush the sides with butter. Set aside until you're ready to bake and serve the torte. (*The torte can be refrigerated, well wrapped, overnight, but bring it to room temperature before heating.*)

6. When you're ready to serve the torte, preheat the oven to 400°F (205°C).

7. Put the torte on a sheet pan or directly on an oven rack and bake until the top and sides are crisp and the torte is warm, about 20 minutes. Sprinkle the torte with the reserved herbs, cut into wedges, and serve.

BUCKWHEAT BLINI

*Makes 36
silver dollar–size blini*

¾ cup plus 1 tablespoon (200 grams) crème fraîche, homemade (page 337) or store-bought, or sour cream

2 teaspoons crumbled fresh (cake) yeast or ¾ teaspoon instant dry yeast

½ teaspoon sugar

½ cup plus 1 tablespoon (85 grams) buckwheat flour (see page 17)

¼ cup plus 2 tablespoons (89 milliliters) whole milk

1 tablespoon (14 grams) unsalted butter, plus more for cooking the blini

¾ teaspoon kosher salt

1 large egg, separated

You will feel very fancy with a plate of these little savory pancakes before you. Like the Gentleman's Torte (page 305), the blini are made with all buckwheat flour, giving them a distinctive flavor and texture (and making them gluten-free). Topped with a little sour cream, dill, and some cured fish or pickled beets (or, of course, caviar), they make an elegant and delicious canapé. Or, with maple syrup and huckleberries, a really cute stack of pancakes.

1. In a medium bowl, whisk together the crème fraîche or sour cream, yeast, and sugar. Stir in the buckwheat flour, cover with plastic wrap, and let stand in a warm place for 30 minutes.

2. In a small saucepan, combine half of the milk and the butter and heat over low heat until the butter melts. Whisk in the remaining milk, then whisk the milk mixture into the buckwheat mixture. Whisk in the salt and egg yolk.

3. In a medium bowl, beat the egg white with a whisk until it holds stiff peaks. With a rubber spatula, fold the beaten egg white into the batter.

4. Heat a 10- or 12-inch (25- or 30.5-centimeter) cast-iron frying pan over medium heat and lightly glaze with butter. Spoon silver dollar–size rounds of batter into the pan, without crowding them. Cook until bubbles appear on the tops of the blini and they are browned on the bottom, about 90 seconds. Using a small offset spatula, flip the blini and cook on the second side until browned, about 30 seconds more. Transfer to a wire rack and repeat with the remaining batter, greasing the pan with additional butter as needed.

5. Serve warm. The blini are best eaten shortly after being made, but they'll keep, refrigerated in an airtight container, overnight. Rewarm in a low oven before eating.

Sourdough Starter: Getting Started, and Care and Feeding

Much has been written about sourdough starters, so I'll give you only the details you actually need to know and not get too philosophical about it. The character of your starter has more to do with the natural yeasts that live in your geographic area than with anything else. The dominant culture is going to dominate your culture; you will be assimilated. That said, keep your commercial yeast the hell away from your starter! Native yeasts are much more delicate than the concentrated yeast made in a factory.

Since it does take a few days to get a new starter ready for action, I encourage bakers to share with each other. It is much easier, and less wasteful, to maintain an active starter than to begin anew, so go fishing and see if you've got a friend or coworker who loves to bake! But even if you do have your grandmother's starter, disasters befall us all from time to time. Many years ago, after a well-meaning assistant threw out the starter (saying "It smelled weird!") given to me by my mentor, Kevin Farmer, I was brokenhearted, having brought it all the way to California from North Carolina. Luckily, good ole *Lactobacillus sanfranciscensis* made herself a new baby when I left a container of flour and water on the counter overnight. Making a starter is really that easy.

You'll note that in all the recipes in this book that call for sourdough starter, it's measured by weight, not volume. If you've resisted getting a digital scale up until this point, now it's time. Because starters increase and decrease in volume depending on how long it has been since they were fed, volume is not an accurate way to measure: It's grams or bust!

Here's how to make a sourdough starter.

Combine 250 grams all-purpose flour and 250 grams warm (90°F/30°C) water in a plastic quart container or bowl and mix to combine. Let stand at room temperature for 1 to 2 hours, then cover and let rest at warm room temperature overnight (between 75°F and 80°F/25°C and 27°C is ideal, but if it's colder, don't worry—it'll still work; if it's much warmer, it'll also still work—just much faster!)

The next day, return to your starter. Remove and discard about three-quarters of the mixture (you can eyeball it, or you can weigh it and discard).

Add another 250 grams all-purpose flour and 250 grams warm water to the starter that remains and stir to combine. Let stand uncovered at room temperature for a couple hours, then cover and let rest in a warm place overnight.

On Day 3, you're going to repeat the same steps you did on Day 2, discarding and feeding the starter, then leaving it to rest.

By Day 4, your starter should have grown and be quite bubbly, and it may have a sour smell; this is normal. Remove and discard all but 100 grams of the starter, then feed the remaining starter with 225 grams all-purpose flour and 250 grams warm water. Cover and let rest in a warm place overnight.

By the end of Day 5, the starter should be ready: Now you're moving from making a starter to maintaining it, with regular feedings that give that wild yeast something to eat. Discard all but 150 grams of the starter, then add 90 grams all-purpose flour and 100 grams warm water to the remaining starter and mix to incorporate. Cover and let rest in a warm place. By the afternoon, the starter should be bubbly.

I use a hydration of 50 percent water and 45 percent flour for all the recipes in this book, which means, dear reader, that when feeding your starter, you must weigh it on your digital scale, then multiply that number by 50 percent to get the amount of water it wants and multiply that same number by 45 percent to get the weight of the flour it wants. Add the water first, and then the flour. Mix the crap out of it by hand. It's fun!

You can keep the starter in a lidded container in the fridge for a long time without killing it, but if you haven't used it in a while, take it out of the fridge and feed it (with 50 percent water and 45 percent flour, the amounts determined by the weight of your starter) a couple of times before trying to bake with it, and let it proof for a couple of hours after the final feeding before using it. Before these feedings to awaken a sleepy starter, be sure to discard a portion of it (give some to a pal), or you will have a swimming pool of wild yeast to fit in the fridge.

To determine when your starter is ready to bake with after feeding, put a small amount in a container of water; if it floats, go for it! If not, check it again at 20-minute intervals to see if it's ready. It should have some larger and some smaller foamy bubbles when you look into the container. If you're trying to fit baking into your personal schedule, try feeding it close to your bedtime and letting it stand at room temperature for an hour, then refrigerating it; it may be perfect by the morning.

20TH CENTURY CAFE'S "AUTHENTIC" SAN FRANCISCO BAGELS

Makes 12 bagels

FOR THE DOUGH

1 cup (237 milliliters) water

281 grams sourdough starter (see page 310)

1 tablespoon plus 1 teaspoon honey

1 tablespoon barley malt syrup

5¾ cups (638 grams) bread flour

3 tablespoons (26 grams) baker's special dry milk powder (be sure it is a very finely ground variety, one that looks a little like tapioca flour or cornstarch)

2 teaspoons fine sea salt

Semolina flour or cornmeal for dusting

FOR THE BOILING-WATER BATH

2 tablespoons (30 milliliters) barley malt syrup

1 tablespoon baking soda

1½ teaspoons kosher salt

Sesame seeds, poppy seeds, or nigella seeds (see page 19), or "everything" bagel spice for topping (optional)

I grew up on Lender's bagels, the dense, pallid disks found in the freezer section of most American grocery stores. But after we moved to Santa Cruz when I was ten years old, I discovered the Bagelry bagel shop downtown (it's still around). I always got the Moxie: cream cheese, olives, and scallions on an onion bagel.

Whenever my husband and I visit New York, we fly back as the most hated people on the plane, with our pungent onion bagels from H&H and a stinky bag from Murray's Cheese. When I decided to try my hand at making my own bagels, my favorite baking book was Nancy Silverton's *Breads from La Brea Bakery*, so I used her recipe. My bagels have evolved quite a bit since that first version. The result is what I like to call a San Francisco bagel, very dense and chewy, leavened entirely with sourdough starter.

1. **MAKE THE DOUGH:** In the bowl of a stand mixer fitted with the dough hook, combine the water, starter, honey, and barley malt syrup and mix on low speed until combined. Add the flour and dry milk powder and mix on low for 3 to 4 minutes, until moistened. Remove the bowl from the mixer stand, cover, and let stand for 20 minutes.

2. Return the bowl to the mixer stand, add the salt, and mix on low until smooth, about 7 minutes (you can do all the mixing by hand, but it's a tremendous workout). Transfer to the refrigerator and let rest for at least 1 hour, or up to 4 hours. If you let it rest for more than an hour, let it stand for a few minutes at room temperature before shaping, which will make it easier to do.

3. Remove the dough from the fridge and portion into 12 pieces (about 3½ ounces/100 grams each). Working with one piece of dough at a time, shape each one into a tight little boule (a fancy baking word for dough ball), using your unfloured work surface to create tension (never use flour for this!): With your dominant hand, make a cage over the piece of dough, letting the heel of your hand rest lightly on the dough, and begin moving your hand in a clockwise direction, applying gentle pressure to the dough; you should feel surface tension developing and notice the dough begin to smooth and tighten. If it is just sliding around and not sticking at all to the counter, wipe the surface with a lightly dampened towel to help create

the necessary tension. The surface of each boule should be very taut, perfectly round, and sealed at the bottom.

4. When all the pieces of dough have been rolled into balls, lightly dust a sheet pan with semolina flour or cornmeal. Roll each ball into a 7-inch (18-centimeter) snake on an unfloured surface. One at a time, wrap each snake into a tight circle around your hand, pinching the overlapping parts together, then set your snake-covered hand palm side down on your dampened work surface and roll back and forth over the seam to seal it. I guarantee that your last bagel will look better than your first! Place the bagels on the prepared sheet as you shape them. Cover the pan with plastic wrap and refrigerate overnight.

5. When you are ready to bake the bagels, remove them from the fridge and let stand at warm room temperature until proofed, 45 minutes to 1 hour. To test if the bagels have proofed enough, fill a deep container with cold water. Push a bagel to the bottom of it; if it bobs up to the top, it's ready. If it remains sunken or rises to the top very slowly, dry it off, return it to the sheet pan, and let the bagels proof longer.

6. When the bagels have proofed, preheat the oven to 400°F (205°C).

7. **PREPARE THE BOILING-WATER BATH:** In a large pot, combine 2 quarts (1.9 liters) water, the barley malt syrup, baking soda, and salt and bring to a boil. Dust a sheet pan with semolina flour or cornmeal and set nearby (if you are coating both sides of the bagels with seeds, you don't need to dust the pan with anything). If you're making seeded (or everything) bagels, pour the seeds (or seed mix) into a rimmed dish (a cake pan or pie plate also works well). Set out a clean tea towel.

8. Poach the bagels in the boiling water in batches, about 30 seconds per side. With a spider or slotted spoon, remove the bagels one at a time from the boiling water and, working quickly, place bottom side down on the tea towel, lift and place top side down in your seed plate, lift again, and then either place the bottom side in the seeds or leave it naked and place the bagel on the prepared sheet pan.

9. Bake until golden brown, 20 to 25 minutes. Cool on the pan.

RUSSIAN BLACK BREAD

Makes 1 large loaf

352 grams sourdough starter (see page 310)

1 cup plus 2 tablespoons (267 milliliters) cold-brewed coffee (see New Orleans Iced-Coffee Float, page 185) or just leftover coffee from the morning

3 tablespoons (45 milliliters) water

3 tablespoons (45 milliliters) blackstrap molasses

2 tablespoons (30 milliliters) honey

2 slightly heaping cups (250 grams) bread flour, plus more for dusting

2¼ cups (240 grams) rye flour

1 tablespoon Dutch-process cocoa powder

2 tablespoons poppy seeds (see page 20)

2½ teaspoons cracked fennel seeds

2 teaspoons caraway seeds, lightly toasted

1½ teaspoons nigella seeds (see page 19)

1 tablespoon fine sea salt

Semolina flour or cornmeal for dusting

As a budding line cook at Pyewacket Restaurant in Chapel Hill, North Carolina, I started in the pantry station, practically slicing off my finger on a mandoline my first day. One of the dishes I was responsible for was smoked-trout pâté with Russian black bread. Of course we bought the bread, and I have no idea how it was made or where it came from, but this is my homage to that bread, and to Muskle, my real first chef, not the chef who let a first-timer in the kitchen slice onions on a mandoline.

This black bread gets its color and deep, rich flavor from coffee, cocoa, and molasses, and a little from the nigella seeds. If you bake this bread often and you don't eat all the bread butts, you can add ⅓ cup (50 grams) of ground toasted black bread, soaked in 3 tablespoons (45 milliliters) water, to the dough to make it just a little bit darker—and reduce waste too! With or without the old bread, the color is a beautiful dark walnut brown. The bread is sweet and delicious topped with butter or cream cheese. Although this recipe calls for a stand mixer, the dough is so wet that it can easily be mixed by hand.

1. In the bowl of a stand mixer fitted with the dough hook, combine the starter, coffee, water, molasses, and honey and mix on low speed to blend. In a large bowl, whisk together the flours, cocoa, and poppy, fennel, caraway, and nigella seeds. With the mixer on low, add the dry ingredients and mix until moistened and sticky, 2 to 3 minutes. Remove the dough hook, cover the bowl, and let stand at room temperature for 20 minutes.

2. Reattach the dough hook, add the salt to the dough, and mix on low for 3 minutes, or until the dough is smooth and elastic. Place in a large ungreased bowl (or a lidded container that can hold three times its current volume), cover with plastic wrap, and let rise at room temperature until doubled, 2 to 3 hours.

3. Vigorously punch the dough down, removing as much air as possible, cover again, and refrigerate overnight.

4. The next day, remove the dough from the refrigerator, turn out onto a lightly floured work surface, and spread out gently. Pull the two opposite sides away from each other, making two "wings." Fold the right side over to the middle and the left wing to the middle, overlapping the right wing.

(continued)

Using both hands, pull the top edge up and away from your body just a bit, then fold it over and down to the middle, sealing it against the dough. Then grab the bottom and pull it up and over to the top. Using both hands, tuck and drag the dough down toward you to create tension on the outside of the dough, spin the dough on the work surface, and continue dragging the dough until it is a uniform round boule, with a smooth outside, free of tears or bulges. Dust the dough lightly with flour. Let rest at room temperature for 10 minutes.

5. Dust a sheet pan with semolina flour or cornmeal. Using a bench scraper, scoop up the dough and turn it flour side down on your work surface. Using your fingertips, gently press the dough down. Lightly moisten your hands with water. Lift the dough up off your work surface and slap it back down again. Repeat a second time; the dough should now be a rough triangular shape. Beginning at the tip of the triangle farthest away from you, roll the dough tightly toward you, pinching as you roll; when you get to the end, gently pinch again, forming a seam to seal the loaf closed. Turn the loaf seam side down and gently roll to elongate it. Transfer to the prepared sheet pan.

6. Set the pan on the top rack of your turned-off oven. Pour boiling water into a baking pan and set it on the rack beneath the bread. Proof the loaf until your fingerprint holds in the dough when it is lightly pressed with a flour-coated finger, 30 to 45 minutes; if it springs back immediately, it's not ready.

7. When the dough is almost proofed, remove the loaf from the oven and preheat the oven to 400°F (205°C).

8. When the oven is hot, sift a light dusting of bread flour over the loaf. With a serrated knife, cut a few horizontal slashes in the top of the loaf. Bake for 45 to 50 minutes, until the crust is browned and the interior temperature reads 205°F to 210°F (95°C to 100°C) on an instant-read thermometer (because this loaf is so dark in color, the internal temperature is the key to judging doneness). Let cool on a wire rack before slicing. The bread will keep for up to 4 days, loosely wrapped in a plastic bag.

PUMPKIN-SEED RYE BREAD

Makes 1 large loaf

352 grams sourdough starter
(see page 310)

1¼ cups (296 milliliters) water

3½ cups (402 grams) bread
flour, plus more for dusting

¾ cup (77 grams) rye flour

¼ cup plus 2 tablespoons
(50 grams) raw pumpkin seeds
(see headnote)

2 teaspoons caraway seeds,
lightly toasted

2 teaspoons fine sea salt

Semolina flour or cornmeal for
dusting

Pumpkin seeds play a big part in Viennese cuisine, and rye bread is found all over eastern and central European menus, both historic and new. I use Styrian pumpkin seeds, a hull-less variety primarily grown in the Styrian region of Austria, because they are extra delicious; the ones we use at the cafe come from an organic farm in southern Oregon. This recipe is based on the first sourdough I ever made, for Elaine's in Chapel Hill, North Carolina, but it was inspired by bread I tasted in Vienna, at one of my favorite restaurants on earth, Zum Schwarzen Kameel. I increased the hydration of the original Elaine's dough and added rye, pumpkin seeds, and caraway. This is a pretty lightweight version of a rye bread, but it has a pleasing loft that makes it an excellent sandwich bread; it was developed specifically for 20th Century Cafe's Reuben. Although the recipe calls for a stand mixer, this dough can easily be mixed by hand.

1. In the bowl of a stand mixer fitted with the hook attachment, combine the starter and water and mix on low speed to blend. In a large bowl, whisk together the flours and pumpkin and caraway seeds. With the mixer on low, add the dry ingredients and mix until moistened and sticky, 1 to 2 minutes. Remove the bowl from the mixer, cover, and let stand at room temperature for 20 minutes.

2. Attach the bowl to the mixer stand, add the salt, and mix on low for 2 to 3 minutes, until the dough is smooth and elastic. Place in a large ungreased bowl (or a lidded container that can hold three times its current volume), cover with plastic wrap, and let rise at room temperature until doubled, 2 to 3 hours.

3. Vigorously punch the dough down, removing as much air as possible, cover again, and refrigerate overnight, or for up to 2 days.

4. The next day, remove the dough from the refrigerator, turn out onto a lightly floured work surface, and spread out gently. Pull the two opposite sides away from each other, making two "wings." Fold the right side over to the middle and the left wing to the middle, overlapping the right wing. Using both hands, pull the top edge up and away from your body just a bit, then fold it over and down to the middle, sealing it against the dough. Then grab the bottom and pull it up and over to the top. Using both

CHALLAH

Makes 1 loaf

100 grams sourdough starter (see page 310)

8 large egg yolks

3½ tablespoons (52 milliliters) canola oil, plus more for greasing the bowl

2 tablespoons (30 milliliters) water

2 tablespoons (30 milliliters) honey

1 tablespoon crumbled fresh (cake) yeast or 1 teaspoon instant dry yeast

2¾ cups (325 grams) bread flour

2 tablespoons (24 grams) sugar

2 teaspoons kosher salt

1 large egg, beaten with 2 teaspoons water, for egg wash

Nigella seeds, poppy seeds, and sesame seeds for topping (optional)

Sharing a delicate cotton candy–like structure with its buttery non-pareve cousin brioche, this egg-rich challah dough is made with oil, rendering it suitable for observant meals. The word "challah" actually refers to the dough offering, which is separated from the mass of dough before the loaf is formed.

I once lost my mind trying to figure out how to do the eight-strand braid that was described in the *Tassajara Bread Book*. I found it (my mind) later, but I have stuck to three- or four-strand braided loaves ever since. For the four-strand braid, all you need is this little ditty from Adam Marca, a great baker, starting from the right: over-under-over. Repeat until your bread is braided!

For Rosh Hashanah, I make a special apple challah, omitting the 2 tablespoons (30 milliliters) water in the dough and replacing it with ¼ cup (60 milliliters) apple puree. I shape it in the traditional single-strand spiral and insert thin slices of apple into the proofed loaf just after the egg wash, before it goes into the oven. Once it cools, I glaze the challah with honey.

1. In the bowl of a stand mixer fitted with the dough hook, combine the starter, egg yolks, oil, water, honey, and yeast and mix on low speed until blended. With the mixer still on low, add the bread flour and mix for about 3 minutes, until a smooth, sticky ball forms. Remove the hook, cover the bowl, and let stand for 20 minutes.

2. Add the sugar and salt to the bowl, reattach the hook, and mix on low speed for about 8 minutes, until very smooth. Transfer the dough to a lightly oiled large bowl and turn to coat on all sides, then cover with plastic wrap and let stand in a warm place until doubled, 1 to 2 hours.

3. Punch the dough down, cover the bowl again, and refrigerate overnight.

4. The next day, turn the dough out onto your work surface. Divide the mass of dough into 3 (or 4) even pieces and shape each piece into a ball. Then, using your palms, roll and stretch each piece into a rope 18 inches (46 centimeters) long, slightly tapering both ends of the rope. Lay the ropes side by side, spacing them 1 inch (2.5 centimeters) apart. Gently pinch them together at the top, then tightly braid the strands. When you

reach the end of the strands, pinch them together and tuck the pinched end under.

5. Transfer the loaf to a sheet pan and let stand in a warm place until very poufy, about 35 minutes; when you press the dough gently with your fingertip, it should hold the impression.

6. While the loaf proofs, preheat the oven to 350°F (175°C).

7. With a pastry brush, brush the challah all over with egg wash; dust the top with seeds, if using. Bake until the loaf is deep golden brown and an instant-read thermometer inserted in the center of the loaf registers 190°F (90°C), 25 to 30 minutes. Let cool on a wire rack before slicing.

VARIATION

French Toast

Challah makes exceptional French toast. First you need to make a custard (this recipe makes 5 cups/1.18 liters of custard, enough for a whole loaf of challah).

1. In a medium saucepan, combine 2 cups (473 milliliters) whole milk and 1 cup (237 milliliters) heavy cream. Split a vanilla bean lengthwise and scrape out the seeds; add the seeds and pod to the milk mixture. Heat until bubbles appear at the edges of the pan, then remove from the heat, cover, and let stand for 1 hour.

2. In a medium bowl, whisk together 2 large eggs, 2 large egg yolks, and 3 tablespoons (36 grams) sugar. Remove the vanilla pod from the milk mixture (rinse the pod with water and save; it can be used to make vanilla sugar) and whisk the mixture into the eggs. Strain the custard through a fine-mesh strainer into a shallow dish (9 by 13 inches/23 by 33 centimeters or similar) if you will be making the French toast right away, or into a storage container if you will be making it the next day, or the day after.

Refrigerate the custard if not making the French toast now, then pour into a shallow dish when ready to proceed.

3. Cut the challah into ¾-inch (2-centimeter) slices and arrange as many slices as will fit in a single layer in the custard. Let soak for 5 minutes, then flip and soak on the second side for 3 or so minutes more, until the bread is saturated. Cook the soaked slices of challah on a buttered griddle or in a buttered frying pan, flipping once, until golden brown on both sides. Repeat with the remaining slices. Serve hot, with sour cream or crème fraîche and maple syrup.

COMPOUND CREAMS AND SAUCES

Many of the desserts in this book are so special that they require nothing more than a pretty platter to serve them on, but few of them would become overwrought with a little gussying up. Think of your favorite black dress: The cut may be perfect and flattering on you, but adding your grandmother's brooch is what makes you a standout at the dinner party.

So here we have a chapter of sweet accessories: compound creams, sauces, and other little finishing touches, plus a few tips on how to use them. I also describe how to create your own unique desserts simply by pulling a few components from different chapters and putting them together. Whether it's pushing your most showstopping dessert up and over the top or just adding a different twist to something you've served your family many, many times, here you'll find the tools you'll need to elevate even the most humble dessert.

Any technique used to flavor a cream in this chapter can be applied to a custard sauce or ice cream. I can't guarantee that you'll love all of your experiments, but if you keep the ingredient ratios in mind and follow the rules given here, you will be able to make innovations that may surprise and delight you, and that will make you a little braver the next time you feel like straying from the beaten path.

Part of the allure of these creams as an accompaniment is their delicate simplicity. Keep in mind that if you do whip them ahead, the creams will start to pick up odors from the fridge, so use them up in a day or two, before they lose their luster.

Skills and Equipment

There are two things that will cause your cream to fail—and one of them is a matter of opinion, but since you asked—not thoroughly chilling your cream before you whip it, and overwhipping the cream (which I've seen done on purpose). Perfectly whipped cream has a shine to it, it's not grainy, and it holds a nice mound when gently dolloped onto a plate. It does not weep or slump! It also does not keep its perfect texture for long—and don't get smart with me, thinking you can overwhip it to somehow keep it stable longer. Overwhipping will cause little fat globules (goblins) to form in your cream, and they will not go away. You can whip the cream in advance, though, and then give it another quick turn with the whisk just before serving.

For the recipes in this chapter, you really need only a bowl and a whisk. I use a mortar and pestle to smash spices and grind up fragrant leaves with sugar, but you can use a blender. A fine-mesh strainer is a big help for removing any bits that might intrude on your ethereal creams; I've used a tea strainer in a bind too! Otherwise, a good arm and a chilled bowl are all you need to make your fluffy little clouds of cream.

WHIPPED CREAM
(20th Century Cafe Schlag)

*Makes 2 cups
(473 milliliters)*

1 cup (237 milliliters) heavy cream

1½ teaspoons sugar

This most basic whipped cream (aka Schlag), just as plain as can be, can accompany any cake you bake and myriad other desserts. You can make it a few hours ahead, and rewhip it right before serving.

In the bowl of a stand mixer fitted with the whisk attachment (or in a large bowl, using a balloon whisk), combine the cream and sugar and beat on medium-high speed until the cream holds soft peaks. Use immediately, or cover and refrigerate for up to 2 days; rewhip before serving.

VANILLA CREAM

*Makes 2 cups
(473 milliliters)*

½ vanilla bean (save the other half for another purpose)

Scant 2 teaspoons sugar

1 cup (237 milliliters) heavy cream

Are you not perplexed by the fact that one of the world's most distinctive—and expensive—spices has somehow become synonymous with "plain"? It makes me indignant. This vanilla cream is elegant and delicious. It is a classic pairing with a strawberry shortcake (see page 46), and it would also be my first choice with the Esterházy Schnitten (page 125) or the Dobos Torta (page 131).

1. With a paring knife, cut the vanilla bean lengthwise in half, then scrape out the seeds and add the seeds and pod to a small saucepan. Pour in the sugar and use your fingertips to rub the sugar into the inside of the bean, extracting any remaining seeds or oil.

2. Pour in the cream and heat over medium heat until it is warm to the touch. Let cool slightly, then transfer to a bowl and let steep in the fridge until cold.

3. Remove the vanilla bean pod from the cream, squeezing out any goodness that has clung to it (you can rinse the bean and save it to make vanilla sugar). Transfer the chilled cream to the chilled bowl of a stand mixer fitted with the whisk attachment (or use a large bowl and a balloon whisk) and whip on medium-high speed until it holds soft peaks. Use immediately, or cover tightly and refrigerate for up to 2 days; rewhip before serving.

ROSE GERANIUM CREAM

Makes 2 cups
(473 milliliters)

A handful of fresh rose geranium leaves, washed and patted dry (see page 19)

2 teaspoons sugar

1 cup (237 milliliters) heavy cream

When I first began to take baking seriously as an occupation, my boss, pastry chef Kathy Edwards, told me to purchase Lindsey Shere's now-classic book, *Chez Panisse Desserts*. Lindsey's book cast a spell on me, with her perfect recipes, its bursting appendix, and her fondness for rose geranium.

Years later, when I was working as a pastry cook at Chez Panisse, we would take rose geranium from the post office next door, which had a giant bush growing right out front!

Unwhipped, this infused cream is ideal for pouring over warm servings of cobblers, crisps, or crumbles, such as the Apricot-Cherry Cobbler (page 45). Whipped, it's a surprising accompaniment to tarts, cakes (think Meyer Lemon Pudding Cake, page 69), and shortcakes, or a component in an ice cream dessert. You can even turn this into a very simple but elegant dessert by layering fresh berries macerated in a tiny bit of sugar in a glass with the cream.

1. Put the rose geranium leaves in a blender and blend on high speed, creating a rose geranium tornado, until they are very finely chopped. Add the sugar and continue blending until the sugar pulls some of the oil and juice from the leaves. Add the cream and pulse on very low speed just a few times to get the color and flavor into the cream. Transfer to a bowl, cover, and refrigerate for at least 1 hour, or up to 1 day.

2. Strain the cream. If using as a pouring cream, pour the chilled infused cream over individual servings of your chosen dessert. Or, to whip the cream, pour the chilled cream into the chilled bowl of a stand mixer fitted with the whisk attachment (or use a large bowl and a balloon whisk) and beat on medium-high speed until soft peaks form. Use immediately, or cover tightly and refrigerate for up to 2 days; rewhip before serving.

LEMON VERBENA CREAM

*Makes 2 cups
(473 milliliters)*

1 cup (237 milliliters) heavy cream

2 teaspoons sugar

A handful of fresh lemon verbena leaves (see page 19)

This cream is very easy to make: Lemon verbena leaves are steeped in hot cream, then the cream is strained and chilled. Crack open a Chocolate Soufflé (page 177) and pour it in, serve a whipped dollop with Strawberry Ice Cream (page 193) and Chocolate Sauce (page 339), or use it for a simple light dessert, layered with fresh blueberries and crushed Cacao Nib Meringue Kisses (page 207). You can also omit the sugar in this recipe and use the infused cream instead of plain cream for your Chocolate Truffles (page 230). Any unused lemon verbena leaves make a wonderful tisane or iced herbal tea.

1. Combine the cream and sugar in a medium saucepan and heat over medium heat until bubbles begin to appear at the edges, then add the lemon verbena leaves, remove from the heat, cover, and let stand for 30 minutes at room temperature, or refrigerate for up to 1 day. Strain when the flavor pleases you and chill thoroughly.

2. If using it as a pouring cream, pour the chilled cream over individual servings of your chosen dessert. Or, to whip the cream, pour the chilled cream into the chilled bowl of a stand mixer fitted with the whisk attachment (or use a large bowl and a balloon whisk) and beat on medium-high speed until it holds soft peaks. Use immediately, or cover tightly and refrigerate for up to 2 days; rewhip before serving.

MEYER LEMON CREAM

*Makes about 1½ cups
(355 milliliters)*

¾ cup (178 milliliters) heavy cream

¼ cup to ½ cup (60 to 120 milliliters) lemon curd, homemade (recipe follows) or store-bought

Pinch of kosher salt, or to taste

Though this Meyer lemon cream is not quite as simple to whip up as some of the other compound creams in this chapter, I promise that it is worth it. (And it is simple if you use store-bought lemon curd!) You can use it to fill little tart shells for a lighter version of a lemon tartlet, or to fill cream puffs, or place a generous dollop alongside each serving of your Strawberry Tart (page 39) or Cranberry-Ginger Upside-Down Cake (page 67).

In the chilled bowl of a stand mixer fitted with the whisk attachment (or in a large bowl, using a balloon whisk), whip the cream on medium-high speed until it holds soft peaks. Fold in the lemon curd, beginning with ¼ cup (57 grams) and then adding more to taste. Season with the salt (the salt will give the cream a little lift) and use right away.

Meyer Lemon Curd

*Makes about 1½ cups
(355 milliliters)*

4 Meyer lemons

2 large eggs

4 large egg yolks

½ cup (99 grams) sugar

10 tablespoons (143 grams) cold unsalted butter, cut into cubes

1. Zest and juice the lemons; set the zest aside. You need about ½ cup (118 milliliters) juice and 3 tablespoons (18 grams) zest.

2. Whisk together the eggs, egg yolks, lemon juice, and sugar in a heat-proof bowl. Set the bowl over a medium saucepan of gently simmering water, making sure the bottom of the bowl doesn't touch the water, and whisk constantly until the mixture is thick and reaches 165°F to 175°F (74°C to 77°C). Pass through a fine-mesh strainer into a large bowl, then whisk in the lemon zest, followed by the butter, adding it a few pieces at a time and whisking until the curd is completely smooth. (If you have an immersion blender, you can spare your arm and use it to incorporate the butter.) Cover with plastic wrap, pressing it directly against the surface of the curd, and refrigerate until thoroughly chilled. Lemon curd will keep, refrigerated, for 2 weeks.

PEACH LEAF CREAM

*Makes about 2 cups
(473 milliliters)*

A handful of fresh peach leaves
(see page 19), washed and
patted dry

1 tablespoon sugar

1 cup (237 milliliters) heavy
cream

You will need to find a friend with a peach or nectarine tree or convince a farmer at the market to bring you some leaves if you want to make this recipe, but the results are impressive. The cream has a distinctive almond flavor and a brilliant green color, and the technique is similar to that for the Peach Leaf Ice Cream (page 182). I like to serve the cream poured over a cobbler, or whip it for a berry and stone fruit shortcake, but it is the very best Schlag for the Mohnkuchen (page 97). For a simplified version, simply heat the cream, steep the leaves until you like the flavor, and strain. In either case, make sure the cream is absolutely COLD before you whip it, or the texture will be terrible.

1. Put the peach leaves in a blender and blend on high speed, creating a peach leaf tornado, until the leaves are very finely chopped. Add the sugar and continue blending until the sugar pulls some of the oil and juice from the leaves. Transfer to a bowl.

2. In a medium saucepan, heat the cream over medium heat until it begins to bubble at the edges of the pan. Pour the hot cream into the bowl with the peach leaf–sugar mixture and whisk like crazy, then quickly pour through a fine-mesh sieve back into the saucepan. Heat over medium heat until just below a boil (this step sets the brilliant green color). Remove from the heat, transfer to a bowl, and let cool to room temperature, then cover and refrigerate until thoroughly chilled.

3. To whip, pour the chilled cream into the chilled bowl of a stand mixer fitted with the whisk attachment (or use a large bowl and a balloon whisk) and beat on medium-high speed until soft peaks form. Use immediately, or cover tightly and refrigerate for up to 2 days; rewhip before serving.

COFFEE-CRUNCH CREAM

*Makes about 2 cups
(473 milliliters)*

1 cup (237 milliliters) heavy cream

2 teaspoons sugar

2 tablespoons whole coffee or espresso beans, crushed

¼ cup (57 grams) chopped Toffee (page 235)

Coffee-infused whipped cream with crushed toffee folded into it is practically a dessert unto itself, but it's a delicious accompaniment to Black Walnut Ice Cream (page 189).

To make the cream, you crush coffee or espresso beans with a rolling pin and steep them in warm cream to extract their flavor. You could also cheat and use half a shot of espresso instead for the coffee flavor.

1. In a medium saucepan, combine the cream and sugar. Add the coffee beans and let steep for 1 hour at room temperature, or up to overnight in the refrigerator.

2. Strain the cream through a fine-mesh sieve into the bowl of a stand mixer fitted with the whisk attachment (or use a large bowl and a balloon whisk) and beat on medium-high speed to soft peaks. Fold in the toffee and serve immediately, before the toffee loses its crunch!

COCONUT CREAM

*Makes about 1¼ cups
(296 milliliters)*

1 cup plus 2 tablespoons
(267 milliliters) heavy cream

½ cup (57 grams) fine dried
unsweetened coconut
(sometimes called macaroon
coconut), toasted

1½ teaspoons sugar

Pinch of kosher salt

This coconut cream is good with so many things—you could do a spoonful alongside a slice of Nectarine Strudel (page 263), Rhubarb Strudel (page 259), or Meyer Lemon Pudding Cake (page 69), or layer it in a glass with raw blueberries and crushed Cacao Nib Meringue Kisses (page 207).

1. In a small saucepan, heat the cream over medium heat until bubbles appear at the edges of the pan. Stir in the toasted coconut, remove from the heat, and let cool, then transfer to a lidded container and refrigerate overnight.

2. Strain the chilled cream through a fine-mesh sieve into the chilled bowl of a stand mixer fitted with the whisk attachment (or use a large bowl and a balloon whisk). Add the sugar and salt and beat on medium speed until soft peaks form. Use immediately, or cover tightly and refrigerate for up to 2 days; rewhip before serving.

CRÈME FRAÎCHE

Makes about 1¼ cups (287 grams)

1 cup (237 milliliters) heavy cream

¼ cup (59 milliliters) buttermilk

2 teaspoons to 1 tablespoon sugar (optional)

Pinch of kosher salt (optional)

This cream can be sweetened and whipped to serve as an accompaniment to myriad desserts, but it also finds a home in the cheesecake recipes (see pages 103 and 105), the rustic tarts (see pages 299 and 302), and the buckwheat crêpe batter (see page 305). And you can beat a little crème fraîche into cream cheese to make it more spreadable on your beautiful bagels (see page 312) or black bread (see page 315).

1. In a large jar or glass bowl, stir together the cream and buttermilk. Cover and set aside at room temperature until thick and tangy but still not sour, 36 to 48 hours. Then transfer to the refrigerator; it will keep for up to 1 week.

2. To whip the crème fraîche for a dessert accompaniment, transfer to the bowl of a stand mixer fitted with the whisk attachment (or use a large bowl and a balloon whisk) and add sugar to taste and the salt. Whip on medium speed to soft peaks. Use immediately, or cover tightly and refrigerate for up to 2 days; rewhip before serving.

VANILLA SAUCE

*Makes about 2 cups
(473 milliliters)*

1 vanilla bean, preferably Madagascar

¼ cup (49 grams) sugar

1 cup (237 milliliters) whole milk

1 cup (237 milliliters) heavy cream

4 large egg yolks

Pinch of kosher salt

This simple, pourable custard sauce (also known as crème anglaise) is rich and delicious, with a wonderful roundness that only a vanilla bean can deliver. I always use Madagascar vanilla beans, because nothing else truly tastes like vanilla to me. I love this with warm Topfen Strudel (page 251) or poured into a hot Chocolate Soufflé (page 177).

1. Split the vanilla bean lengthwise and put it in a medium saucepan with the sugar. Use the sugar and your fingers to exfoliate every bit of vanilla goodness—the seeds, sticky bits, all of it—out of the pod, and leave the pod in the saucepan. Pour in the milk and cream and heat over medium heat until bubbles begin to appear at the edges of the pan. Remove from the heat, cover, and let stand for at least 1 hour or refrigerate overnight.

2. In a medium bowl, beat the egg yolks. Uncover the vanilla cream and return the pan to medium heat. When bubbles begin to appear at the edges of the pan, remove from the heat and whisk about one-quarter of the hot cream mixture into the yolks, then pour the yolk mixture back into the saucepan with the remaining cream. Return to the stove and cook over low heat, stirring constantly, until the sauce coats the back of a spoon. If the cream was very hot, this will happen in a flash, so pay attention!

3. Remove from the heat and taste the cream: If the vanilla flavor is strong enough, strain through a fine-mesh sieve into a clean bowl, stir in the salt, and cool in an ice bath before covering and refrigerating. If you want a more pronounced vanilla flavor, follow the steps for cooling and storing but leave the vanilla bean in overnight; strain just before using. The sauce can be stored in an airtight container in the refrigerator for up to 3 days.

CHOCOLATE SAUCE

*Makes about 1½ cups
(355 milliliters)*

9 ounces (255 grams) 72% cacao chocolate, such as Valrhona Araguani, finely chopped

Scant ¼ cup (55 milliliters) water

Scant ¼ cup (55 milliliters) heavy cream

Pinch of kosher salt, or to taste

Great chocolate makes great chocolate sauce, so don't skimp here.

1. In a medium saucepan, combine the chocolate and water and heat over medium heat, whisking, until the chocolate has melted and the mixture is smooth and homogeneous. Meanwhile, in a small saucepan, heat the cream over medium heat until bubbles appear at the edges of the pan. Whisk the cream into the melted chocolate mixture until smooth, then add the salt.

2. Use the sauce right away, or let cool and refrigerate in a lidded heatproof container until ready to use; it will keep for up to 2 weeks. When ready to serve, reheat the sauce in the container in a water bath (or in the top of a double boiler) until hot and pourable.

TOFFEE SAUCE

*Makes about 1½ cups
(355 milliliters)*

1 cup (198 grams) sugar

9 tablespoons (127 grams) unsalted butter

½ cup plus 1 tablespoon (133 milliliters) heavy cream

¼ teaspoon kosher salt

This sauce is really just toffee extended with cream. If you want to make coffee-toffee sauce, add a splash or two of strong espresso after you add the cream.

1. Combine the sugar and butter in a medium saucepan and cook over medium heat, stirring, until the mixture melts and resembles peanut butter, then let cook, stirring, for a minute or two more, until the mixture begins to smoke. Immediately remove from the heat and continue stirring for 1 minute. Switch to a whisk and carefully whisk in the cream (it will bubble furiously) and the salt.

2. Use the sauce right away, or transfer to a lidded heatproof container, let cool to room temperature, and refrigerate; it will keep for up to a week. To reheat, uncover and warm in the container in a water bath (or in the top of a double boiler) until hot and pourable.

ROSE GERANIUM SYRUP

Makes about ½ cup
(118 milliliters)

½ cup (99 grams) sugar

¼ cup (59 milliliters) water

A few drops of lemon juice

12 rose geranium leaves (see page 19), rinsed and patted dry

This recipe makes quite a bit of syrup, but it's the smallest amount you can really make and still have the blades go round in your blender. You can freeze what you don't need, but it has so many uses! Use it as a plate sauce for apple or rhubarb tarts with Cardamom Ice Cream (page 180), or add a little along with the sugar when you macerate berries for a strawberry shortcake with Meyer Lemon Cream (page 333). It pairs well with anything containing berries or stone fruit. Use it in a floral version of an Arnold Palmer, or add it to cocktails.

1. Combine the sugar, water, and lemon juice in a medium saucepan and bring to a boil over high heat. Remove from the heat, let cool, and chill until cold.

2. Put the rose geranium leaves in your blender and blend on high speed, making a rose geranium tornado. Add the chilled sugar syrup and continue to blend on high speed until you have a lovely green, fragrant syrup. Transfer to a lidded jar and refrigerate until ready to use.

3. The syrup will keep for 4 days in the refrigerator, although the color will become less vibrant after a few days; it will retain its integrity in the freezer for up to 3 months.

RESOURCES

Almond Flour/Meal
Alfieri Farms
alfierifarms.com

Black Walnuts
Wine Forest Wild Foods
wineforest.com

Cacao Nibs
Valrhona
valrhona-chocolate.com

World Wide Chocolate
worldwidechocolate.com

Chestnut Flour
nuts.com

Chocolate
Chocosphere
chocosphere.com

Valrhona
valrhona-chocolate.com

Dates
Flying Disc Ranch
flyingdiscranch.com

Rancho Meladuco
ranchomeladuco.com

Dried Plums
Blossom Bluff Orchards
blossombluff.com

Gelatin
Modernist Pantry
modernistpantry.com

Nigella Seeds and Poppy Seeds
Penzeys Spices
penzeys.com

Paprika
Red Fangs
red-fangs.com

Rose Water
Nielsen-Massey
nielsenmassey.com

Sourdough Starter
King Arthur Flour
kingarthurflour.com

Tapioca Flour
Bob's Red Mill
bobsredmill.com

Vanilla
Beanilla
beanilla.com

Penzeys Spices
penzeys.com

341

ACKNOWLEDGMENTS

Thanks to:

Mimi Cheng for never judging and for giving me the strength to power through.

Nicole Krasinski, who always sees me through rose-colored glasses.

Samin Nosrat, who released the honey cake secret to the universe and stood by to defend it against poachers.

Aya Brackett, bringer of apricots, limes, and plums from the magic garden, who also brought forth the life and light from this food.

Jessica Battilana, who tested and converted these recipes, fought with me about how much a cup of milk weighs, put software on my computer, and broke quarantine to bring me pozole when I was an invalid.

Danielle Svetcov for finding a willing victim to publish this monsterpiece, and for letting me know when to hold 'em and when to fold 'em.

Steven Lyles for coming to the cafe every day, undaunted by the 20th Century mayhem.

Vivek Bald for punk rock; without it, nothing good would ever follow.

Bret Jennings and Phil West for giving me a chance and letting me have my own way.

Hayden Ashley for making me believe that I am a chef worthy of respect.

Caitlin McCormick (Fancy), Adam Marca, and Hili Rezvan for being the keepers of my recipes ("Don't worry, guys; I'll remember this") and sending them to me when the time came. How we gonna have a book without recipes?

Martin Bournhonesque, gentleman farmer, for marvelous dinner parties and beautiful vegetables, and for being the very best neighbor.

Emily Luchetti, Alice Medrich, and Rick Rodgers for the kind words.

Judy Pray, Lia Ronnen, Bella Lemos, Sibylle Kazeroid, Judith Sutton, Suet Chong, Nancy Murray, Allison McGeehon, Theresa Collier, Amy Michelson, and all the gang at Artisan for betting on a newcomer, and for managing to get this book out in spite of a pandemic and my cancer.

Ben Kunst, who brought me to the Old World and helped me bring a piece of it to life here in San Francisco.

My parents for unleashing me onto this planet, and my sister, who eventually forgave me for ruining her sixth birthday.

Katharine Kunst, Katherine Fulton, Ezra Pearlman, Theresa Sweeny, James Blanchard, Mike and Tana Powell, Bruce Hill, Staffan Terje, Matthew and Stacy Perry, Allison and Dan Rose, Joe Sum, Greg Alsterlind, Charles Hemminger, and Pam Mendelsohn for making the 20th Century Cafe possible.

INDEX

MICHELLE POLZINE, chef/owner of 20th Century Cafe, is one of San Francisco's most talented pastry chefs. She began cooking in North Carolina in 1992, got her big break in 1995 at Chapel Hill's Pyewacket restaurant, and has since worked at some of Bay Area's best restaurants, including Delfina, Chez Panisse, and Range. The work of this James Beard Award–nominated pastry chef has been featured in *Bon Appétit*, *Food & Wine*, the *San Francisco Chronicle*, and the *New York Times*, among other publications. She lives with her husband and cats in San Francisco. Follow her on Instagram at @20thcenturycafesf.